W9-BLU-036

FOREWORD

This little book introduces you to the greatest legal document ever written: the United States Constitution.

The Constitution is certainly the most influential legal document in existence. Since its creation some two hundred years ago, over one hundred countries around the world have used it as a model for their own.

And it is a living document. It is one of the world's oldest surviving constitutions. And, while the Supreme Court continually interprets the Constitution so as to reflect a rapidly changing world, its basic tenets have remained virtually unchanged since its inception, and unchallenged as well. People quarrel over its interpretation, but never do they question the wisdom of its underlying principles. Imagine creating a document that governs your grandchildren's grandchildren's grandchildren! That's what the men of the 1787 Constitutional Convention did.

For this very reason, great people have spent their lives studying and interpreting the Constitution. In this little book, you'll begin to see why. You'll get a taste of some of the Founding Fathers' thoughts. You'll see some of the reasoning behind the Supreme Court's landmark decisions. But, most importantly, you'll get a feel for the Constitution itself and how it is that a document that was written over 200 years ago still plays an integral role in our everyday lives.

"The Constitution is the guide, which I never will abandon."

— GEORGE WASHINGTON

THE U.S. CONSTITUTION

And Fascinating Facts About It

Supplemental text by Terry L. Jordan

EIGHTH EDITION
Second Printing

About the Author: Terry Jordan received a B.S. in Education from Taylor University and a master's in History from Cleveland State University. He has spent much of his life studying, interpreting and teaching students about the U.S. Constitution. Terry recently retired after a thirty-five-year career as a public school teacher. Thirty-two of those years he spent at Orange High School in Pepper Pike, Ohio, where he taught Advanced Placement United States History. Terry lives in Solon, Ohio, with his wife, Linda, and three children, Lea, Cali, and Cody. This book is dedicated to Bob and Helen Jordan and Jim and "Boots" Freeman.

Copyright ©2013 by Oak Hill Publishing Company. All rights reserved. No part of this publication may be reproduced or transmitted in any form or by any means, electronic or mechanical, including photocopy, recording, or any information storage and retrieval system, without permission in writing from the publisher.

ISBN-10: 1-891743-15-5; ISBN-13: 978-1-891743-15-3

Library of Congress Catalog Card Number: 2012930766

Also available in Spanish

Published by: Oak Hill Publishing Company
Box 6473, Naperville, IL 60567

Printed in the United States of America

∞ *The U.S. Constitution And Fascinating Facts About It* is printed on acid-free paper, which preserves the contents, reduces yellowing, and helps protect the environment.

For Individual Copies Of This Book:
Visit your local bookstore or www.ConstitutionFacts.com

For Wholesale, Government, Bulk Orders, Corporate or Educational Sales: Call 1-800-887-6661

www.ConstitutionFacts.com

TABLE OF CONTENTS

THE U.S. CONSTITUTION

THE DECLARATION OF INDEPENDENCE

THE ARTICLES OF CONFEDERATION

THE SUPREME COURT

THE FOUNDING FATHERS

The U.S. Constitution brought together, in one remarkable document, ideas from many people and several existing documents, including the Articles of Confederation and Declaration of Independence. Those who made significant intellectual contributions to the Constitution are called the "Founding Fathers" of our country.

Many of the Founding Fathers were at the Constitutional Convention, where the Constitution was hammered out and ratified. George Washington, for example, presided over the Convention. James Madison, also present, wrote the document that formed the model for the Constitution.

Other Founding Fathers were not there, but made significant contributions in other ways. Thomas Jefferson, who wrote the Declaration of Independence, was serving as ambassador to France at the time of the Convention. He kept abreast of the proceedings in Philadelphia by carrying on correspondence with James Madison. John Adams, as ambassador to Great Britain, wrote "Defense of the Constitution of the Government of the United States Of America." Thomas Paine wrote the influential pamphlet "Common Sense," which immeasurably influenced the philosophy reflected in the Declaration of Independence. One of the Founding Fathers, Patrick Henry, was initially opposed to the very idea of the Constitution! He wanted to keep the Articles of Confederation, the predecessor to the Constitution. However, when an agreement was made to add a "bill of rights" to the Constitution, Henry fought hard for its ratification.

The term "framers" is sometimes used to specify those who helped "craft" the Constitution. "Founding Fathers" often refers to people who contributed to the development of independence and nationhood. However, the notion of a "framer" or a "Founding Father" is not easily defined. When the following sections of the book talk about "Founding Fathers," they are describing people who had a significant impact on the Constitution either directly or indirectly. The list is by no means complete, but it does identify people who played a large role in the development of the Constitution at this crucial time in American history.

FASCINATING FACTS
ABOUT SIX FOUNDING FATHERS

GEORGE WASHINGTON (1732-1799)

Highest Political Office: President (1789-1797)

Other Accomplishments: Led the colonial forces in the Revolutionary War.

The staid portraits of George Washington accurately reflect the personality of the father of the nation. He was a man of few words, whose political ascension was attributable to his strength of character, rather than his intellect.

A huge man for his day, Washington stood 6'3½" tall with enormous hands. Washington had pockmarked skin as a result of a teenage case of smallpox, and a shy disposition that was the result of a domineering mother. Twice he proposed to women, and twice he was rejected. He finally married Martha Custis, the richest widow in Virginia.

He had lost almost all his teeth by the time he was president, leaving him with badly sunken cheeks that were stuffed with cotton for portraits. Contrary to popular belief, George Washington never had wooden teeth! His teeth were made mostly of lead fitted with human, cattle, and hippopotamus teeth. Some were carved from elephant and walrus tusks.

In his will, he freed all 300 of his slaves permanently. The popular tale of Washington and the cherry tree, historians say, was almost certainly untrue.

His Politics: Washington was a Federalist, so he favored a strong central government. He also had a strong affinity for aristocrats. During the Constitutional Convention, he spent much of his time at the mansion of Robert Morris, the richest man in America. His closest political ally was Alexander Hamilton, whose policies inevitably leaned toward the upper classes.

Washington was the only president to win unanimous approval (all of the votes cast) by the electoral college. He did it twice.

In office, Washington served the nation best by keeping the government stable. He advocated a strong national defense, and kept the country out of the escalating tension between England and France.

His health failing, Washington begged out of the presidency after one term. Men from both sides of the political fence urged him to remain in office, however, so he stayed on. His second inaugural address may reveal his enthusiasm for the second term. At 133 words, it is the shortest inaugural address in history.

Closest Crony Among the Founding Fathers: Alexander Hamilton

What He Said: "Government is not reason, it is not eloquence—it is a force! Like fire, it is a dangerous servant and a fearful master; never for a moment should it be left to irresponsible action."

JAMES MADISON (1751-1836)

Highest Political Office: President (1809-1817)

Other Accomplishments: Helped draft Virginia's state constitution when he was 25. Virginia's constitution later became the model for the U.S. Constitution. Served as Jefferson's Secretary of State.

Madison was a soft-spoken and tiny man—about 5'4" and less than 100 pounds. Even his nickname was diminutive: "Jemmy." He was too small to serve in the Revolutionary War, and turned to politics instead.

Madison, "the Father of the Constitution"—the most important legal document in modern history—never received a law degree.

Even in his forties, Madison was a lonely and single man. That changed when Aaron Burr introduced him to Dolley Todd. The couple married when Madison was 43, and never had children.

Dolley Madison earned a place in history when she stole away from the White House with crucial government documents and a portrait of George Washington as the British stormed the capital during the War of 1812.

Madison outlived all of the other Founding Fathers. He died at the age of eighty-five in June 1836.

His Politics: His presidency was marred by the War of 1812—the only war in which U.S. soil was overrun by enemy forces. The war was precipitated by the widespread sentiment that the United States was destined to conquer Canada, then a British territory.

Aside from the war that nearly cost him his reelection, Madison's two terms were also memorable for the fact that both of his vice presidents died while in office.

Closest Crony Among the Founding Fathers: Jefferson and Madison were close friends throughout their lives: Madison was Jefferson's protégé. After their presidencies, each spent many days at the other's estate. Jefferson named one of the bedrooms at Monticello "Mr. Madison's room."

What He Said: On the War of 1812: "I flung forward the flag of the country, sure that the people would press onward and defend it."

Under the new Constitution, the nation's powers will be "derived from the superior power of the people."

THOMAS JEFFERSON (1743-1826)

Highest Political Office: President (1801-1809)

Other Accomplishments: Wrote the Declaration of Independence, and served as Minister to France (a pivotal diplomatic position) as the Constitution was being drafted.

Jefferson was nicknamed "Long Tom" because he stood 6'2 ½" tall, with long, slender limbs. He had carrot-red hair that paled with age. A fiddle player, Jefferson wooed his wife with violin serenades. Jefferson eschewed the uniforms of nobility, choosing instead to dress himself in sometimes dirty and tattered clothing. Although his wife died at the age of 33, Jefferson never remarried. He did, however, allegedly father five children by Sally Hemings, one of his slaves. Jefferson suffered from migraine headaches throughout his life, and bathed his feet in cold water daily to avoid colds. He was the quintessential Renaissance man and has been described as a: lawyer, linguist, diplomat, astronomer, naturalist, political philosopher, educator, statesman, president, farmer, musician, scientist, inventor, agriculturalist, horseman, geographer, theologian, and paleontologist. Jefferson was fluent in Greek, Latin, French, Spanish, Italian, and German. He was a supporter of equal rights and education for women, the right of all to have a free public education, a free library system, and the creation of a decimal system of weights and measures. He is also considered one of the preeminent architects in the history of the country.

His Politics: Jefferson was a Republican, which at that time was the party of the common man. He envisioned a nation built on agriculture, not industry. The formal name for the "Republican" Party was the Democratic-Republican Party from which our present day Democratic Party evolved. (The Republican Party of today was created in 1854 by the joining of anti-slavery Democrats, the Free Soil Party, and factions of the Whig Party.) The formal name of the opposing party (led by Alexander Hamilton) was the Federalist Party.

Jefferson was renowned for being a terrible public speaker due to a speech impediment, although he is certainly regarded as one of the most gifted writers ever to hold the office of the presidency. He alone wrote the first draft of the Declaration of Independence.

He doubled the land size of the United States when he made the Louisiana Purchase from Napoleon. Napoleon needed cash to conquer Europe; Jefferson wanted the land to safeguard against a future French invasion and to encourage his vision of America being a land of small, independent (yeoman) farmers. The selling price: $15 million.

After his two terms as president, Jefferson retired to his Virginia estate, Monticello. He spent much of his time pursuing his dream of establishing a university. That dream was realized when he founded the University of Virginia.

Closest Crony Among the Founding Fathers: Although his closest friend among the founding fathers was James Madison, Jefferson's most memorable friendship was with John Adams. The friendship developed when they both worked on the committee that was responsible for the Declaration of Independence. Their friendship turned to a bitter rivalry, however, when they joined opposing political parties. They reconciled after both finished their presidencies, and they kept up a steady correspondence. They both died on July 4, 1826—the 50th anniversary of the Declaration of Independence. On the day he died, Adams opened his eyes and whispered his last words: "Thomas Jefferson lives." Jefferson had died earlier that day.

What He Said: "A little rebellion now and then is a good thing." "Science is my passion, politics my duty."

JOHN ADAMS (1735-1826)

Highest Political Office: President (1797-1801)

Other Accomplishments: First vice president. Helped draft the Declaration of Independence and negotiate the peace agreement with Great Britain to end the Revolutionary War. Served as Minister to Great Britain.

Nicknamed "Atlas of American Independence," John Adams was a short (5'7"), plump man with an ego as big as his waistline. He felt it was beneath him to shake hands with anyone; he bowed instead. Adams was not alone in this practice, however. George Washington also preferred to bow rather than shake hands.

Born and raised in what is now Quincy, Massachusetts, Adams was a lawyer by trade. He was the first president to occupy the White House. The nation moved its capital from Philadelphia to Washington, D.C., during his administration.

His Politics: Adams was a Federalist, and, as such, he held a more elitist view of government than his Republican rivals.

The first truly defense-minded president, Adams built the U.S. Navy to the point where it could compete with that of any nation.

Probably his most enduring political legacy involved appointing John Marshall as Supreme Court Chief Justice; the most ignominious, his signing of the "Alien and Sedition Acts," which made it a crime to criticize the government (for which violators could be imprisoned).

Adams was most proud of the fact that he avoided war with France at the turn of the century, in the face of strong public opinion in favor of war. This, along with his perceived overspending on defense, led to his defeat in his reelection campaign.

Closest Crony Among the Founding Fathers: Thomas Jefferson was, by turns, both his closest crony and most loathed political enemy. They ended their lives as friends, dying on the same day, 50 years after the signing of the Declaration of Independence (see Fascinating Facts about Thomas Jefferson).

What He Said: "Let the human mind loose. It must be

loosed. It will be loose. Superstition and despotism cannot confine it."

BENJAMIN FRANKLIN (1706-1790)

Highest Political Office: Minister to France

Other Accomplishments: Franklin was one of the three Americans to sign the peace treaty with England that ended the Revolutionary War. He also helped write the Declaration of Independence, and was the oldest delegate at the Constitutional Convention.

Of the Founding Fathers, Franklin was easily the most unusual character. He made enough money from his publishing business—primarily on receipts from *Poor Richard's Almanack*—to retire at age 42. He then devoted his life to writing, science, and politics.

Among his many inventions, Franklin created bifocal glasses. He did so because he didn't like to carry two pairs of glasses with him.

Franklin had one illegitimate son, William, who became the governor of New Jersey. William supported the British in the Revolution, which resulted in the permanent estrangement of father and son.

His Politics: Franklin's political activism had peaked long before the American party system fully evolved, but he was philosophically closest to the tenets of the Democratic-Republican party.

He was suspicious of strong central governments and governors, be they kings or presidents. Indeed, Franklin advocated a three-person presidential committee rather than having a single president. Of the proposal to have a one-man president, he said, "The government is likely to be well-administered for a course of years, and can only end in despotism." Nonetheless, in Franklin's will, he bequeathed his walking stick to President Washington.

Franklin had a restless and ravenous mind. He eschewed normal work patterns, preferring instead to set his own pace, and ignore appointments if he was interested enough in a conversation. He also possessed the largest private library in America.

Not all of his ideas won wide acceptance. A case in point: Franklin's choice for the national bird was the turkey.

Closest Crony Among the Founding Fathers: Thomas Jefferson. When Franklin died, Jefferson implored President Washington to hold a day of mourning. Washington balked, not wishing to set a precedent.

What He Said: "Our Constitution is in actual operation. Everything appears to promise that it will last. But in this world nothing is certain but death and taxes." At the conclusion of the Constitutional Convention Franklin observed the symbol of the sun at the top of George Washington's chair and mused: "I have the happiness to know it is a rising sun and not a setting sun."

ALEXANDER HAMILTON (1755-1804)

Highest Political Office: Treasury Secretary

Other Accomplishments: Along with Madison and John Jay, authored the "Federalist Papers," rallying support for the new Constitution. Led the effort to convene the Constitutional Convention when the nation was verging on anarchy.

Hamilton called for a meeting of all 13 states at Annapolis, Maryland, in September 1786 to discuss the economic situation in the country at that time. However, only five states sent representatives. There were not enough states for a quorum, and the conference had no real authority. Undaunted, Hamilton then requested permission from the Congress of the Confederation (under the Articles of Confederation) to invite representatives from the thirteen states to assemble in Philadelphia with the express purpose of "revising" the Articles of Confederation. With the exception of Rhode Island, all of the states sent representatives. Behind closed doors and with no real authority, the delegates decided to write an entirely new constitution.

Hamilton was consumed by his passion for a nation built around a strong and fiscally stable central government. He was born out of wedlock in the West Indies, and moved to the colonies at the age of 17. His father, a Scottish trader, went bankrupt when Hamilton was 15, and the boy went to work in a counting house to help support the family.

Fresh out of Columbia University, Hamilton organized artillery regiments in New York for the Revolutionary

War, and from 1779 to 1781 he was Washington's chief aide. When Washington assumed the presidency, he named Hamilton Secretary of the Treasury.

Ironically, before Washington was elected president, Hamilton was one of a group of politicians who felt that the U.S. needed a king. The group wrote to Prussia's Prince Henry and asked if he wanted the job. Before he replied, the group changed its mind.

His Politics: Hamilton was the one who most advocated an elitist political vision. He believed that the intellectual aristocracy should rule the nation.

Hamilton's political legacy is embodied in the Federal Bank. He led the effort to establish the first such bank, which he saw as critical for sustaining the government's fragile finances. His opponents saw the bank as an evil tool for expanding the power of the federal government, at the expense of the states. Hamilton is regarded as the "Father of the National Debt" because he felt that a national debt was really a "blessing." The more money the government owed to the people of the country, the more the people had a stake in the success of the country!

When Jefferson ran for president in 1800, he and Aaron Burr (both Republicans) tied. The election went to the Federalist-controlled House. Hamilton, founder of the Federalist Party, convinced his colleagues to elect Jefferson over Burr. Burr then campaigned for governor of New York in 1804. Again, Hamilton swayed voters against Burr. Finally, Burr challenged Hamilton to a duel. Fatally wounded by his rival, Hamilton died one day later.

Closest Crony Among the Founding Fathers: George Washington.

What He Said: "The sacred rights of mankind are not to be rummaged for among old parchments or musty records. They are written, as with a sunbeam, in the whole volume of human nature, by the hand of the Divinity itself, and can never be erased or obscured by mortal power."

MORE FASCINATING FACTS ABOUT THE FOUNDING FATHERS

★★★★★

George Washington was born on February 11, 1731, under the Julian calendar. In the early 1750s, Great Britain converted to the Gregorian calendar. An act of Parliament added eleven days to complete the adjustment, and Washington's birthday became February 22, 1732!

★★★★★

Once Gouverneur Morris was offered a bet of one dinner if he would approach George Washington, slap him on the back, and give him a friendly greeting. He wanted to show people how "close" he was to the "chief." Morris carried out the bet, but later admitted that after seeing the cold stare from Washington, he wouldn't do it again for a thousand dinners!

★★★★★

Of the Founding Fathers who became president, only George Washington did not go to college. John Adams graduated from Harvard, James Madison graduated from Princeton, and Thomas Jefferson attended the College of William and Mary.

★★★★★

John Adams was the first president to live in the White House when he came to Washington, D.C., in November of 1800. However, he was only there for four months after losing the election of 1800 to Thomas Jefferson.

★★★★★

Washington Irving described James Madison as "a withered little applejohn" and his wife Dolley as a "fine, portly, buxom dame."

★★★★★

The Marquis de Lafayette thought so much of George Washington that he named his son George Washington Lafayette.

★★★★★

George Washington gave the shortest inauguration speech in American history on March 4, 1793. It was only 133 words long. William Henry Harrison gave the longest at 8,443 words on March 4, 1841, on a cold and blustery day in Washington, D.C. He died one month later of a severe cold.

★★★★★

John Adams died on July 4, 1826, at the age of 90 years, 247 days. He had the longest marriage of any ex-president. He and Abigail were married October 25, 1764, and the marriage lasted 54 years (his wife died in 1818).

★★★★★

Upon graduating from Harvard, John Adams became a grammar school teacher. "My little school, like the great world, is made up of Kings, politicians, divines, fops, buffoons, fiddlers, fools, coxcombs, sycophants, chimney sweeps, and every other character I see in the world. I would rather sit in school and consider which of my pupils will turn out to be a hero, and which a rake, which a philosopher and which a parasite, than to have an income of a thousand pounds a year."

★★★★★

Thomas Jefferson sometimes spent $50 a day (about $944 today) for groceries because of his lavish entertaining. The wine bill for the eight years he served as president was $11,000 (about $208,000 today!). He was also the first president to grow tomatoes in North America.

★★★★★

Thomas Jefferson died broke. Before his death, Jefferson was able to alleviate part of his financial problems by accepting $25,000 for his books from Congress. Those books were used to begin the Library of Congress. Friends even tried to organize a lottery to sell part of his land to help, but it was not enough.

★★★★★

When Jefferson died, he left "my gold mounted walking staff of animal horn as a token of cordial and affectionate friendship" to James Madison. Jefferson's epitaph read: "Here was buried Thomas Jefferson, author of the Declaration of Independence, of the statute of Virginia for Religious Freedom, and the father of the University of Virginia." It didn't include "President of the United States"!

★★★★★

James Madison of Virginia was responsible for proposing the resolution to create the various Cabinet positions within the Executive Branch of our government and twelve amendments to the Constitution, of which ten became the Bill of Rights. He also proposed that congressional pay be determined by the average price of wheat during the previous six years of a congressional session!

★★★★★

Although it is common knowledge that George Washington called for the emancipation of his slaves in his last will and testament, he stipulated that it would only take place upon the death of his wife, Martha. However, in Martha's will she did not free the slaves.

★★★★★

The original intent was for George Washington to be buried beneath the Rotunda floor under the dome of the Capitol. He died before the Rotunda was finished, and in 1828 the crypt was covered up.

★★★★★

President George Washington would bow to guests at presidential receptions to avoid physical contact. This tradition lasted through the presidency of John Adams. Washington would rest one hand on a sword while holding a hat in the other to avoid the remote possibility of anyone forcing a handshake! Thomas Jefferson ended the tradition of "bowing" by shaking hands when greeting people.

★★★★★

Thomas Jefferson at eighty-three years of age felt that he would not live through the summer of 1826, but he hoped to live through July 4th (the 50th anniversary of the Declaration of Independence). Both he and John Adams died on July 4, 1826, after long and distinguished careers. They had earlier been friends, then political enemies, and by the end of their lives had maintained a steady correspondence. Adams' last words were: "Thomas Jefferson lives," not knowing that Jefferson had expired earlier that day in Virginia. Jefferson's last words were: "Is it the Fourth? I resign my spirit to God, my daughter, and my country."

★★★★★

President James Monroe also died on July 4th. He died on July 4, 1831—five years after Thomas Jefferson and John Adams.

★★★★★

When George Washington died on December 14, 1799, his last words were: "I die hard, but I am not afraid to go ... Let me go quietly. I cannot last long ... It is well."

★★★★★

Alexander Hamilton was killed by Aaron Burr in a duel in Weehawken, New Jersey, on July 12, 1804. Hamilton's son, Philip, had died in a duel three years earlier (1801) at the same location.

★★★★★

Benjamin Franklin died on April 17, 1790. His daughter asked him to change positions on his bed to improve his breathing and his last words were: "A dying man can do nothing easy."

★★★★★

Benjamin Franklin died on April 17, 1790, at the age of 84. The 20,000 mourners at his funeral on April 21, 1790, constituted the largest public gathering up to that time.

SIGNERS OF THE CONSTITUTION

(The 39 delegates who signed the Constitution and what happened to them after 1787.)

On September 17, 1787, the Constitutional Convention came to a close in the Assembly Room of Independence Hall in Philadelphia, Pennsylvania. There were seventy individuals chosen to attend the meetings with the initial purpose of amending the Articles of Confederation. Rhode Island opted to not send any delegates. Fifty-five men attended most of the meetings, there were never more than forty-six present at any one time, and ultimately only thirty-nine delegates actually signed the Constitution. (William Jackson, who was the secretary of the convention, but not a delegate, also signed the Constitution. John Delaware was absent but had another delegate sign for him.) While offering incredible contributions, George Mason of Virginia, Edmund Randolph of Virginia, and Elbridge Gerry of Massachusetts refused to sign the final document because of basic philosophical differences. Mainly, they were fearful of an all-powerful government and wanted a bill of rights added to protect the rights of the people.

The following is a list of those individuals who signed the Constitution along with a brief bit of information concerning what happened to each person after 1787. Many of those who signed the Constitution went on to serve more years in public service under the new form of government. The states are listed in alphabetical order followed by each state's signers.

State and Signers
CONNECTICUT

William S. Johnson *(1727-1819)*—He became the president of Columbia College (formerly known as King's College), and was then appointed as a United States Senator in 1789. He resigned from the Senate in 1791 to return to Columbia. He retired from education in 1800.

Roger Sherman *(1721-1793)*—He campaigned strongly

for the ratification of the Constitution and served as a United States Representative (1789-1791) and Senator (1791-1793) until his death in 1793 at the age of 72.

DELAWARE

Richard Bassett *(1745-1815)*—He was appointed as a United States Senator from Delaware (1789-1793), and was instrumental in the organization of the Judiciary of the United States. He favored moving the nation's capital from New York City to Washington, D.C., and was opposed to Alexander Hamilton's plan of the assumption of state debts by the federal government. After his retirement from the Senate, he devoted the rest of his life to public affairs in Delaware. He was elected governor of Delaware (1799-1801).

Gunning Bedford, Jr. *(1747-1812)*—President Washington appointed him the first United States district judge for the state of Delaware in 1789, a position he held until his death in 1812.

Jacob Broom *(1752-1810)*—Broom became the first postmaster of Delaware from 1790-1792, and was the head of the board of the Delaware Bank of Wilmington. He was involved in business ventures such as operating a cotton mill and running a machine shop, and was involved with attempts to improve the infrastructure of the state of Delaware in such areas as toll roads, canals, and bridges. He also served on the board of the College of Wilmington and showed concern for many other philanthropic activities.

John Dickinson *(1732-1808)*—He lived for twenty years after the official ratification of the Constitution but held no public offices. He spent much of his time writing about politics, and criticized the administration of President John Adams. He died in 1808 at the age of 75. Thomas Jefferson wrote: "A more estimable man or truer patriot could not have left us ... It has been a great comfort to me to have retained his friendship to the last moment of his life."

George Read *(1733-1798)*—He served for four years as a United States Senator (1789-1793), and became the first chief justice of Delaware in 1793.

GEORGIA

Abraham Baldwin *(1754-1807)*—He served in the House of Representatives (1789-1799), and was appointed for two terms to the United States Senate (1799-1807). He died before completing his second term.

William Few *(1748-1828)*—He was appointed as a United States Senator from Georgia (1789), and was defeated for his seat in 1795. He moved to New York in 1799 and was elected to the state legislature in 1801. From 1804-1814 he was the director of the Manhattan Bank and the president of City Bank.

MARYLAND

Daniel Carroll *(1730-1796)*—He served one term in the United States House of Representatives (1789-1791), and was appointed by President George Washington to oversee the construction of the federal capital on the Potomac River. Washington, D.C., is situated on one of his farms.

Daniel Jenifer of St. Thomas *(1723-1790)*—He did not really take an active part in the development of the Constitution. He and the other delegate from Maryland oftentimes voted against each other. He did, however, campaign for the Constitution's ratification and afterwards retired from public life.

James McHenry *(1753-1816)*—After the Convention McHenry went back to his home state and served in various positions of the state legislature (1789-1796) and was appointed Secretary of War by President George Washington (1796-1800). He proved rather ineffectual in this position, and President John Adams called for his resignation in 1800. He retired from public office, and in 1812 was stricken with paralysis in both legs. He was bedridden for the remainder of his life.

MASSACHUSETTS

Nathaniel Gorham *(1738-1796)*—When the Constitutional Convention was finished, Gorham retired from public life. He got heavily into land speculation in New York, but his overindulgence eventually got him into deep financial trouble. He suffered from apoplexy and died a poor man in 1796.

Rufus King *(1755-1827)*—He was a member of the ratification convention in Massachusetts but moved to New

York and became a United States Senator (1789-1795; 1813-1825). He failed to win the Federalist Party's nomination for president in 1816, but was appointed Minister to England in 1824.

NEW HAMPSHIRE

Nicholas Gilman *(1755-1814)*—He was elected to the United States House of Representatives (1789-1797), and was a United States Senator (1805-1814).

John Langdon *(1741-1819)*—He served as a United States Senator for twelve years (1789-1801), and served as governor of New Hampshire from 1805-1812 (with the exception of the year 1809).

NEW JERSEY

David Brearly *(1745-1790)*—He lived only three years after the end of the Constitutional Convention. He was a main supporter of the Constitution at the New Jersey ratifying convention, and President Washington rewarded him with an appointment as a federal district judge. Brearly was active in the Masonic Order in New Jersey and the Society of the Cincinnati (an organization of former Revolutionary War officers).

Jonathan Dayton *(1760-1824)*—He served in the United States House of Representatives from 1791 to 1799, and was chosen Speaker of the House for four years. He became a United States Senator (1799-1805), and was a close acquaintance of Aaron Burr. Dayton was indicted in 1807 for treason along with Burr in a plot to combine Mexico and the Western Territories of the United States. His (Dayton's) case was never brought to trial.

William Livingston *(1723-1790)*—He helped in the ratification fight for the Constitution and served as the governor of New Jersey until his death in 1790.

William Paterson (Patterson) *(1745-1806)*—He was appointed to the United States Senate (1789-1790), and was also appointed by President George Washington as a justice of the United States Supreme Court (1793) until his death.

NEW YORK

Alexander Hamilton *(1755-1804)*—After the Convention, Hamilton worked with John Jay and James

Madison on a series of articles known as the "Federalist Papers" as propaganda for the Constitution. He served as the first United States Secretary of the Treasury from 1789 to 1795. He retired to his law practice and was later appointed to the position of Major General from 1798 to 1800 during an impending war with France. When Hamilton helped defeat Aaron Burr's quest for the governorship of New York, Burr challenged Hamilton to a duel. He was killed by Burr on July 12, 1804.

NORTH CAROLINA

William Blount *(1749-1800)*—Although he signed the Constitution, that action was taken just to prove that he was "present." He supported its ratification because it would help Western expansion, and he used various elected positions to gain land for his own economic advancement. Blount served as state senator (1788-1790), governor of the territory south of the Ohio River (1790), president of the Tennessee constitutional convention (1796), and as a United States Senator from Tennessee (1796-1797). Blount was involved in a conspiracy for inciting the Creek and Cherokee Indians to collaborate with the British Fleet in attacking Spanish Florida and Louisiana. Based upon these charges Blount was impeached by the House of Representatives and expelled by the Senate in 1797. He returned to Tennessee and served in the state senate.

Richard D. Spaight *(1758-1802)*—He was elected to three terms as governor of North Carolina beginning in 1792, and was a major force in moving the capital from New Bern to Raleigh. He was elected a member of the United States House of Representatives (1798-1801) and was killed in a duel by his successor in Congress (John Stanly) in 1802.

Hugh Williamson *(1735-1819)*—He was elected to two terms in the United States House of Representatives (1789-1793), and then retired from public life. He spent many of his remaining years at the New York Hospital, dedicating much of his time to the study of medicine. One of his chief interests was writing on the climate of North America.

PENNSYLVANIA

George Clymer *(1739-1813)*—He was elected to the United States House of Representatives (1789-1791) and became involved in civic and cultural activities in and around Philadelphia. He served as the president of the Bank of Philadelphia.

Thomas Fitzsimons *(1741-1811)*—Fitzsimons served as a member of the United States House of Representatives (1789-1795) and strongly supported the financial plan of Secretary of the Treasury Alexander Hamilton. When he left Congress, he spent the remainder of his life in private business, and served as president of the Philadelphia Chamber of Commerce. Fitzsimons was concerned with religious affairs, public education, and served as trustee of the University of Pennsylvania.

Benjamin Franklin *(1706-1790)*—At the same time that Franklin was attending the Constitutional Convention, he was also the president of the Pennsylvania Society for Promoting the Abolition of Slavery (1787). Harvard, Yale, St. Andrews, William and Mary, and Oxford all granted him honorary degrees. He died in 1790 at the age of eighty-four.

Jared Ingersoll *(1749-1822)*—He served as Attorney General of Pennsylvania from 1790 to 1799, and also as city solicitor of Philadelphia from 1789 to 1801. He ran as the vice presidential candidate under George Clinton in the election of 1812 against James Madison and Elbridge Gerry and lost. He then served as the presiding judge of the district court of Philadelphia from 1821 to 1822.

Thomas Mifflin *(1744-1800)*—He was elected the first governor of Pennsylvania in 1790 and held that position until 1799. He also served as a major general and commander-in-chief of the Philadelphia militia.

Gouverneur Morris *(1752-1816)*—He was appointed by President George Washington as the United States Commissioner to England (1790-1791) and the United States Minister to France (1792-1794). He became a United States Senator (1800-1803), and was the chairman of the Erie Canal Commission (1810-1813). His last elected position was that of president of the New York Historical Society (1816).

Robert Morris *(1734-1806)*—Morris was chosen as the first United States Senator from Pennsylvania and served in that position from 1789 to 1795. President George

Washington asked him to become the first Secretary of the Treasury but he declined the position and recommended Alexander Hamilton instead. After governmental service, Morris was deeply involved in land speculation in the District of Columbia and in Ohio. He was the "Richest Man in America" but met financial ruin and spent three years in debtor's prison. Morris died penniless in 1806.

James Wilson *(1742-1798)*—Wilson returned to Pennsylvania after the Constitutional Convention and played a major role in its successful ratification. He served on the United States Supreme Court (1789-1798) and as a professor of law at the University of Pennsylvania. He was deeply involved in questionable land deals and soon got himself in severe financial difficulty. While visiting a fellow Supreme Court justice, James Iredell in Edenton, North Carolina, Wilson had a nervous breakdown. He died a pauper in 1798.

SOUTH CAROLINA

Pierce Butler *(1744-1822)*—He was appointed one of the state's first two senators (1789) and served until he resigned in 1796. He was appointed a seat in the United States Senate in 1803 but resigned (again) before the end of his appointment in 1804.

Charles Pinckney *(1757-1824)*—He was elected governor of South Carolina (1789-1792; 1796-1798; 1806- 1808), and also served as a United States Senator (1798-1801). He resigned his senate seat to become minister to Spain from 1801-1809, served in the South Carolina state legislature (1810-1814), and then became a member of the House of Representatives from 1819-1821 where he adamantly opposed the Missouri Compromise.

Charles Cotesworth Pinckney *(1746-1825)*—He served as the United States Minister to France during the administration of George Washington and was part of the mission to France during the so-called "XYZ Affair." It was Pinckney who said at the time, "Millions for defense, sir, but not one cent for tribute!," and upon his return to the United States he began to prepare for a war with France with former President Washington and Alexander Hamilton. However, the situation was resolved before it could come to that. He ran unsuccessfully for the vice presidency as the Federalist candidate along with John Adams in 1800. Pinckney also lost his bid for the presidency against Thomas Jefferson in 1804 and James Madison in 1808.

John Rutledge *(1739-1800)*—Rutledge was appointed an Associate Justice of the Supreme Court (1789-1791). He was then appointed Chief Justice of the Supreme Court in 1795, but was not confirmed because of his negative feelings toward the Jay Treaty.

RHODE ISLAND

Rhode Island did not send any delegates to the Constitutional Convention.

VIRGINIA

John Blair *(1732-1800)*—His accomplishments were overshadowed by contributions of James Madison, but his support for the Constitution was rewarded by President George Washington with an appointment to the United States Supreme Court in 1789. He served in that position until his retirement due to ill health in 1796.

James Madison *(1751-1836)*—When the work of the Constitutional Convention was completed, Madison went on to play a major part in its ratification process by joining John Jay and Alexander Hamilton in writing the "Federalist Papers." He became a member of the House of Representatives (1789-1797), was United States Secretary of State (1801-1809), and President of the United States (1809-1817). He outlived all of the other Founding Fathers.

George Washington *(1732-1799)*—Washington served for eight years as the first President of the United States under the new Constitution. His first four years were dominated by domestic issues and the second four years by foreign policy issues. During the administration of President John Adams there was a threat of war with France, and again, Washington came back to serve his country in the capacity of Commander-in-Chief. With the threat of war over he went back to live his last days at his beloved Mt. Vernon. He died there on December 14, 1799. At a memorial "Light Horse Harry" Lee said that George Washington was "first in war, first in peace, and first in the hearts of his countrymen."

FASCINATING FACTS
ABOUT THE U.S. CONSTITUTION

★★★★★

The U.S. Constitution has 4,440 words. It is the oldest and the shortest written constitution of any major government in the world.

★★★★★

Of the spelling errors in the Constitution, "Pensylvania" above the signers' names is probably the most glaring.

★★★★★

Thomas Jefferson did not sign the Constitution. He was in France during the Convention, where he served as the U.S. minister. John Adams was serving as the U.S. minister to Great Britain during the Constitutional Convention and did not attend either.

★★★★★

The Constitution was "penned" by Jacob Shallus, a Pennsylvania General Assembly clerk, for $30 ($762 today).

★★★★★

Since 1952, the Constitution has been on display in the National Archives Building in Washington, DC. Currently, all four pages are displayed behind protective glass framed with titanium. To preserve the parchment's quality, the cases contain argon gas and are kept at 67 degrees Fahrenheit with a relative humidity of 40 percent.

★★★★★

Constitution Day is celebrated on September 17, the anniversary of the day the framers signed the document.

★★★★★

The Constitution does not set forth requirements for the right to vote. As a result, at the outset of the Union, only male property-owners could vote. African Americans were not considered citizens, and women were excluded from the electoral process. Native Americans were not given the right to vote until 1924.

★★★★★

James Madison, "the father of the Constitution," was one of the first to arrive in Philadelphia for the Constitutional Convention. He arrived in early May, bearing the blueprint for the new Constitution.

★★★★★

Of the forty-two delegates who attended most of the meetings, thirty-nine actually signed the Constitution. Edmund Randolph and George Mason of Virginia and Elbridge Gerry of Massachusetts refused to sign due in part to the lack of a bill of rights.

★★★★★

When it came time for the states to ratify the Constitution, the lack of any bill of rights was the primary sticking point.

★★★★★

The Great Compromise saved the Constitutional Convention, and, probably, the Union. Authored by Connecticut delegate Roger Sherman, it called for proportional representation in the House, and one representative per state in the Senate (this was later changed to two.) The compromise passed 5-to-4, with one state, Massachusetts, "divided."

★★★★★

Patrick Henry was elected as a delegate to the Constitutional Convention, but declined, because he "smelt a rat."

★★★★★

Because of his poor health, Benjamin Franklin needed help to sign the Constitution. As he did so, tears streamed down his face.

★★★★★

Gouverneur Morris was largely responsible for the "wording" of the Constitution, although there was a Committee of Style formed in September 1787.

★★★★★

The oldest person to sign the Constitution was Benjamin Franklin (81). The youngest was Jonathan Dayton of New Jersey (26).

★★★★★

When the Constitution was signed, the United States' population was 4 million. It is now more than 315 million. Philadelphia was the nation's largest city, with 40,000 inhabitants.

★★★★★

A proclamation by President George Washington and a congressional resolution established the first national Thanksgiving Day on November 26, 1789. The reason for the holiday was to give "thanks" for the new Constitution.

★★★★★

The first time the formal term "The United States of America" was used was in the Declaration of Independence.

★★★★★

It took one hundred days to actually "frame" the Constitution.

★★★★★

There was initially a question as to how to address the President. The Senate proposed that he be addressed as "His Highness the President of the United States of America and Protector of their Liberties." Both the House of Representatives and the Senate compromised on the use of "President of the United States."

★★★★★

James Wilson originally proposed the President be chosen by popular vote, but the delegates agreed (after 60 ballots) on a system known as the Electoral College. Although there have been 500 proposed amendments to change it, this "indirect" system of electing the president is still intact.

★★★★★

George Washington and James Madison were the only presidents who signed the Constitution.

★★★★★

In November of 1788 the Congress of the Confederation adjourned and left the United States without a central government until April 1789. That is when the first Congress under the new Constitution convened with its first quorum.

★★★★★

James Madison was the only delegate to attend every meeting. He took detailed notes of the various discussions and debates that took place during the convention. The journal that he kept during the Constitutional Convention was kept secret until after he died. It (along with other papers) was purchased by the government in 1837 at a price of $30,000 (that would be $649,000 today). The journal was published in 1840.

★★★★★

Although Benjamin Franklin's mind remained active, his body was deteriorating. He was in constant pain because of gout and having a stone in his bladder, and he could barely walk. He would enter the convention hall in a sedan chair carried by four prisoners from the Walnut Street jail in Philadelphia.

★★★★★

As Benjamin Franklin left the Pennsylvania State House after the final meeting of the Constitutional Convention on September 17, 1787, he was approached by the wife of the mayor of Philadelphia. She was curious as to what the new government would be. Franklin replied, "A republic, madam. If you can keep it."

★★★★★

On March 24, 1788, a popular election was held in Rhode Island to determine the ratification status of the new Constitution. The vote was 237 in favor and 2,945 opposed!

★★★★★

The members of the first Congress of the United States included 54 who were delegates to the Constitutional Convention or delegates to the various state-ratifying conventions. The number also included 7 delegates who opposed ratification.

★★★★★

Vermont ratified the Constitution on January 10, 1791, even though it had not yet become a state.

★★★★★

The word "democracy" does not appear once in the Constitution.

★★★★★

There was a proposal at the Constitutional Convention to limit the standing army for the country to 5,000 men. George Washington sarcastically agreed with this proposal as long as a stipulation was added that no invading army could number more than 3,000 troops!

★★★★★

John Adams referred to the Constitution as "the greatest single effort of national deliberation that the world has ever seen" and George Washington wrote to the Marquis de Lafayette that "It (the Constitution) appears to me, then, little short of a miracle."

★★★★★

The Pennsylvania State House (where the Constitutional Convention took place) was where George Washington was appointed the commander of the Continental Army in 1775 and where the Declaration of Independence was signed in 1776. It was also where the Articles of Confederation were adopted as our first constitution in 1781.

★★★★★

To amend the Constitution, a proposal must gain the support of two-thirds of the House and Senate, and three-fourths of the states. As a result, of the thousands of proposed amendments, only 27 have passed. Amendments must be proposed either by a two-thirds vote in Congress, or by Constitutional Convention. Such a convention can only be held if two-thirds of the states' legislatures support it.

★★★★★

During an event to celebrate the Constitution's Sesquicentennial in 1937, Harry F. Wilhelm recited the entire document through the newly added 21st Amendment from memory. He then obtained a job in the Sesquicentennial mailroom!

DATES TO REMEMBER
(The Constitution)

May 25, 1787: The Constitutional Convention opens with a quorum of seven states in Philadelphia to discuss revising the Articles of Confederation. Eventually, all states but Rhode Island are represented.

September 17, 1787: All 12 state delegations approve the Constitution. 39 delegates sign it of the 42 present, and the Convention formally adjourns.

June 21, 1788: The Constitution becomes effective for the ratifying states when New Hampshire is the ninth state to ratify it.

February 4, 1789: The first presidential election takes place but the results will not be known until April 6.

March 4, 1789: The first Congress under the Constitution convenes in New York City.

April 6, 1789: George Washington is elected the first President of the United States under the Constitution with 69 electoral votes. John Adams is elected Vice President with 34 votes.

April 30, 1789: George Washington is inaugurated as the first President of the United States.

June 8, 1789: James Madison introduces the proposed Bill of Rights in the House of Representatives.

September 24, 1789: Congress establishes a Supreme Court, 13 district courts, 3 ad hoc circuit courts, and the position of Attorney General.

September 25, 1789: Congress approves 12 amendments and sends them to the states for ratification.

February 2, 1790: The Supreme Court convenes for the first time.

December 15, 1791: Virginia ratifies the Bill of Rights, and 10 of the 12 proposed amendments become part of the U.S. Constitution.

THE CONSTITUTION OF THE UNITED STATES

The signing of the Constitution took place on September 17, 1787, at the Pennsylvania State House (now called Independence Hall) in Philadelphia.

PREAMBLE

We the People of the United States, in Order to form a more perfect Union, establish Justice, insure domestic Tranquility, provide for the common defence, promote the general Welfare, and secure the Blessings of Liberty to ourselves and our Posterity, do ordain and establish this Constitution for the United States of America.

Article I

THE LEGISLATIVE BRANCH

Section 1. All legislative Powers herein granted shall be vested in a Congress of the United States, which shall consist of a Senate and House of Representatives.

THE HOUSE OF REPRESENTATIVES

Section 2. [1] The House of Representatives shall be composed of Members chosen every second Year by the People of the several States, and the Electors in each State shall have the Qualifications requisite for Electors of the most numerous Branch of the State Legislature.

[2] No Person shall be a Representative who shall not have attained to the Age of twenty-five Years, and been seven Years a Citizen of the United States, and who shall not, when elected, be an Inhabitant of that State in which he shall be chosen.

[3] [Representatives and direct Taxes shall be apportioned among the several States which may be included within this Union, according to their respective Numbers, which shall be determined by adding to the whole Number of free Persons, including those bound to Service for a Term of Years, and excluding Indians not taxed, three fifths of all other Persons.] *(Note: Changed by section 2 of the Fourteenth Amendment.)* The actual Enumeration shall be made within three Years after the first Meeting of the Congress of the United States, and within every subsequent Term of ten Years, in such Manner as they

shall by Law direct. The Number of Representatives shall not exceed one for every thirty Thousand, but each State shall have at Least one Representative; and until such enumeration shall be made, the State of New Hampshire shall be entitled to chuse three, Massachusetts eight, Rhode-Island and Providence Plantations one, Connecticut five, New-York six, New Jersey four, Pennsylvania eight, Delaware one, Maryland six, Virginia ten, North Carolina five, South Carolina five, and Georgia three.

[4] When vacancies happen in the Representation from any state, the Executive Authority thereof shall issue Writs of Election to fill such Vacancies.

[5] The House of Representatives shall chuse their Speaker and other Officers; and shall have the sole Power of Impeachment.

THE SENATE

Section 3. [1] The Senate of the United States shall be composed of two Senators from each State, [chosen by the Legislature thereof,] *(Note: Changed by section 1 of the Seventeenth Amendment.)* for six Years; and each Senator shall have one Vote.

[2] Immediately after they shall be assembled in Consequence of the first Election, they shall be divided as equally as may be into three Classes. The Seats of the Senators of the first Class shall be vacated at the Expiration of the second Year, of the second Class at the Expiration of the fourth Year, and of the third Class at the Expiration of the sixth Year, so that one-third may be chosen every second Year; [and if Vacancies happen by Resignation, or otherwise, during the Recess of the Legislature of any State, the Executive thereof may make temporary Appointments until the next Meeting of the Legislature, which shall then fill such Vacancies.] *(Note: Changed by clause 2 of the Seventeenth Amendment.)*

[3] No Person shall be a Senator who shall not have attained to the Age of thirty Years, and been nine Years a Citizen of the United States, and who shall not, when elected, be an Inhabitant of that State for which he shall be chosen.

[4] The Vice President of the United States shall be President of the Senate, but shall have no Vote, unless they be equally divided.

[5] The Senate shall chuse their other Officers, and also a President pro tempore, in the Absence of the Vice

President, or when he shall exercise the Office of President of the United States.

[6] The Senate shall have the sole Power to try all Impeachments. When sitting for that Purpose, they shall be on Oath or Affirmation. When the President of the United States is tried, the Chief Justice shall preside: And no Person shall be convicted without the Concurrence of two thirds of the Members present.

[7] Judgment in Cases of Impeachment shall not extend further than to removal from Office, and disqualification to hold and enjoy any Office of honor, Trust or Profit under the United States: but the Party convicted shall nevertheless be liable and subject to Indictment, Trial, Judgment and Punishment, according to Law.

ORGANIZATION OF CONGRESS

Section 4. [1] The Times, Places and Manner of holding Elections for Senators and Representatives, shall be prescribed in each State by the Legislature thereof; but the Congress may at any time by Law make or alter such Regulations, except as to the Place of Chusing Senators.

[2] The Congress shall assemble at least once in every Year, and such Meeting shall be [on the first Monday in December,] *(Note: Changed by section 2 of the Twentieth Amendment.)* unless they shall by Law appoint a different Day.

Section 5. [1] Each House shall be the Judge of the Elections, Returns and Qualifications of its own Members, and a Majority of each shall constitute a Quorum to do Business; but a smaller number may adjourn from day to day, and may be authorized to compel the Attendance of absent Members, in such Manner, and under such Penalties as each House may provide.

[2] Each House may determine the Rules of its Proceedings, punish its Members for disorderly Behavior, and, with the Concurrence of two thirds, expel a Member.

[3] Each House shall keep a Journal of its Proceedings, and from time to time publish the same, excepting such Parts as may in their Judgment require Secrecy; and the Yeas and Nays of the Members of either House on any question shall, at the Desire of one fifth of those Present, be entered on the Journal.

[4] Neither House, during the Session of Congress, shall, without the Consent of the other, adjourn for more than three days, nor to any other Place than that in which the two Houses shall be sitting.

Section 6. [1] The Senators and Representatives shall receive a Compensation for their Services, to be ascertained by Law, and paid out of the Treasury of the United States. They shall in all Cases, except Treason, Felony and Breach of the Peace, be privileged from Arrest during their Attendance at the Session of their respective Houses, and in going to and returning from the same; and for any Speech or Debate in either House, they shall not be questioned in any other Place.

[2] No Senator or Representative shall, during the Time for which he was elected, be appointed to any civil Office under the Authority of the United States, which shall have been created, or the Emoluments whereof shall have been encreased during such time; and no Person holding any Office under the United States, shall be a Member of either House during his Continuance in Office.

Section 7. [1] All Bills for raising Revenue shall originate in the House of Representatives; but the Senate may propose or concur with Amendments as on other Bills.

[2] Every Bill which shall have passed the House of Representatives and the Senate, shall, before it become a Law, be presented to the President of the United States; If he approve he shall sign it, but if not he shall return it, with his Objections to that House in which it shall have originated, who shall enter the Objections at large on their Journal, and proceed to reconsider it. If after such Reconsideration two thirds of that House shall agree to pass the Bill, it shall be sent, together with the Objections, to the other House, by which it shall likewise be reconsidered, and if approved by two thirds of that House, it shall become a Law. But in all such Cases the Votes of both Houses shall be determined by Yeas and Nays, and the Names of the Persons voting for and against the Bill shall be entered on the Journal of each House respectively. If any Bill shall not be returned by the President within ten Days (Sundays excepted) after it shall have been presented to him, the Same shall be a Law, in like Manner as if he had signed it, unless the

Congress by their Adjournment prevent its Return, in which Case it shall not be a Law.

[3] Every Order, Resolution, or Vote to which the Concurrence of the Senate and House of Representatives may be necessary (except on a question of Adjournment) shall be presented to the President of the United States; and before the Same shall take Effect, shall be approved by him, or being disapproved by him, shall be repassed by two thirds of the Senate and House of Representatives, according to the Rules and Limitations prescribed in the Case of a Bill.

POWERS GRANTED TO CONGRESS

Section 8. [1] The Congress shall have Power To lay and collect Taxes, Duties, Imposts and Excises, to pay the Debts and provide for the common Defence and general Welfare of the United States; but all Duties, Imposts and Excises shall be uniform throughout the United States;

[2] To borrow money on the credit of the United States;

[3] To regulate Commerce with foreign Nations, and among the several States, and with the Indian Tribes;

[4] To establish an uniform Rule of Naturalization, and uniform Laws on the subject of Bankruptcies throughout the United States;

[5] To coin Money, regulate the Value thereof, and of foreign Coin, and fix the Standard of Weights and Measures;

[6] To provide for the Punishment of counterfeiting the Securities and current Coin of the United States;

[7] To establish Post Offices and post Roads;

[8] To promote the Progress of Science and useful Arts, by securing for limited Times to Authors and Inventors the exclusive Right to their respective Writings and Discoveries;

[9] To constitute Tribunals inferior to the supreme Court;

[10] To define and punish Piracies and Felonies committed on the high Seas, and Offenses against the Law of Nations;

[11] To declare War, grant Letters of Marque and Reprisal, and make Rules concerning Captures on Land and Water;

[12] To raise and support Armies, but no Appropriation of Money to that Use shall be for a longer Term than two Years;

[13] To provide and maintain a Navy;

[14] To make Rules for the Government and Regulation of the land and naval Forces;

[15] To provide for calling forth the Militia to execute the Laws of the Union, suppress Insurrections and repel Invasions;

[16] To provide for organizing, arming, and disciplining the Militia, and for governing such Part of them as may be employed in the Service of the United States, reserving to the States respectively, the Appointment of the Officers, and the Authority of training the Militia according to the discipline prescribed by Congress;

[17] To exercise exclusive Legislation in all Cases whatsoever, over such District (not exceeding ten Miles square) as may, by Cession of particular States, and the acceptance of Congress, become the Seat of the Government of the United States, and to exercise like Authority over all Places purchased by the Consent of the Legislature of the State in which the Same shall be, for the Erection of Forts, Magazines, Arsenals, dock-Yards, and other needful Buildings; —And

[18] To make all Laws which shall be necessary and proper for carrying into Execution the foregoing Powers, and all other Powers vested by this Constitution in the Government of the United States, or in any Department or Officer thereof.

POWERS FORBIDDEN TO CONGRESS

Section 9. [1] The Migration or Importation of such Persons as any of the States now existing shall think proper to admit, shall not be prohibited by the Congress prior to the Year one thousand eight hundred and eight, but a tax or duty may be imposed on such Importation, not exceeding ten dollars for each Person.

[2] The privilege of the Writ of Habeas Corpus shall not be suspended, unless when in Cases of Rebellion or Invasion the public Safety may require it.

[3] No Bill of Attainder or ex post facto Law shall be passed.

[4] No Capitation, or other direct, Tax shall be laid, unless in Proportion to the Census or Enumeration herein before directed to be taken. *(Note: See the Sixteenth Amendment.)*

[5] No Tax or Duty shall be laid on Articles exported from any State.

[6] No Preference shall be given by any Regulation of Commerce or Revenue to the Ports of one State over those of another: nor shall Vessels bound to, or from, one State, be obliged to enter, clear, or pay Duties in another.

[7] No Money shall be drawn from the Treasury, but in Consequence of Appropriations made by Law; and a regular Statement and Account of the Receipts and Expenditures of all public Money shall be published from time to time.

[8] No Title of Nobility shall be granted by the United States: And no Person holding any Office of Profit or Trust under them, shall, without the Consent of the Congress, accept of any present, Emolument, Office, or Title, of any kind whatever, from any King, Prince, or foreign State.

POWERS FORBIDDEN TO THE STATES

Section 10. [1] No State shall enter into any Treaty, Alliance, or Confederation; grant Letters of Marque and Reprisal; coin Money; emit Bills of Credit; make any Thing but gold and silver Coin a Tender in Payment of Debts; pass any Bill of Attainder, ex post facto Law, or Law impairing the Obligation of Contracts, or grant any Title of Nobility.

[2] No State shall, without the Consent of the Congress, lay any Imposts or Duties on Imports or Exports, except what may be absolutely necessary for executing its inspection Laws: and the net Produce of all Duties and Imposts, laid by any State on Imports or Exports, shall be for the Use of the Treasury of the United States; and all such Laws shall be subject to the Revision and Controul of the Congress.

[3] No State shall, without the Consent of Congress, lay any duty of Tonnage, keep Troops, or Ships of War in time of Peace, enter into any Agreement or Compact with another State, or with a foreign Power, or engage in War, unless actually invaded, or in such imminent Danger as will not admit of delay.

Article II

Section 1. [1] The executive Power shall be vested in a President of the United States of America. He shall hold his Office during the Term of four Years, and, together with the Vice-President, chosen for the same Term, be elected, as follows.

[2] Each State shall appoint, in such Manner as the Legislature thereof may direct, a Number of Electors, equal to the whole Number of Senators and Representatives to which the State may be entitled in the Congress: but no Senator or Representative, or Person holding an Office of Trust or Profit under the United States, shall be appointed an Elector.

[3] [The Electors shall meet in their respective States, and vote by Ballot for two persons, of whom one at least shall not be an Inhabitant of the same State with themselves. And they shall make a List of all the Persons voted for, and of the Number of Votes for each; which List they shall sign and certify, and transmit sealed to the Seat of the Government of the United States, directed to the President of the Senate. The President of the Senate shall, in the Presence of the Senate and House of Representatives, open all the Certificates, and the Votes shall then be counted. The Person having the greatest Number of Votes shall be the President, if such Number be a Majority of the whole Number of Electors appointed; and if there be more than one who have such Majority, and have an equal Number of Votes, then the House of Representatives shall immediately chuse by Ballot one of them for President; and if no Person have a Majority, then from the five highest on the List the said House shall in like Manner chuse the President. But in chusing the President, the Votes shall be taken by States, the Representation from each State have one Vote; a quorum for this Purpose shall consist of a Member or Members from two thirds of the States, and a Majority of all the States shall be necessary to a Choice. In every Case, after the Choice of the President, the Person having the greatest Number of Votes of the Electors shall be the Vice President. But if there should remain two or more

who have equal Votes, the Senate shall chuse from them by Ballot the Vice-President.] *(Note: Superseded by the Twelfth Amendment.)*

[4] The Congress may determine the Time of chusing the Electors, and the Day on which they shall give their Votes; which Day shall be the same throughout the United States.

[5] No person except a natural born Citizen, or a Citizen of the United States, at the time of the Adoption of this Constitution, shall be eligible to the Office of President; neither shall any person be eligible to that Office who shall not have attained to the Age of thirty-five Years, and been fourteen Years a Resident within the United States.

[6] [In Case of the Removal of the President from Office, or of his Death, Resignation, or Inability to discharge the Powers and Duties of the said Office, the same shall devolve on the Vice President, and the Congress may by Law, provide for the Case of Removal, Death, Resignation or Inability, both of the President and Vice President, declaring what Officer shall then act as President, and such Officer shall act accordingly, until the Disability be removed, or a President shall be elected.] *(Note: Changed by the Twenty-Fifth Amendment.)*

[7] The President shall, at stated Times, receive for his Services, a Compensation, which shall neither be encreased nor diminished during the Period for which he shall have been elected, and he shall not receive within that Period any other Emolument from the United States, or any of them.

[8] Before he enter on the Execution of his Office, he shall take the following Oath or Affirmation: —"I do solemnly swear (or affirm) that I will faithfully execute the Office of President of the United States, and will to the best of my Ability, preserve, protect and defend the Constitution of the United States."

Section 2. [1] The President shall be Commander in Chief of the Army and Navy of the United States, and of the Militia of the several States, when called into the actual Service of the United States; he may require the Opinion in writing, of the principal Officer in each of the executive Departments, upon any subject relating to the

Duties of their respective Offices, and he shall have Power to Grant Reprieves and Pardons for Offenses against the United States, except in Cases of Impeachment.

[2] He shall have Power, by and with the Advice and Consent of the Senate, to make Treaties, provided two-thirds of the Senators present concur; and he shall nominate, and by and with the Advice and Consent of the Senate, shall appoint Ambassadors, other public Ministers and Consuls, Judges of the supreme Court, and all other Officers of the United States, whose Appointments are not herein otherwise provided for, and which shall be established by Law: but the Congress may by Law vest the Appointment of such inferior Officers, as they think proper, in the President alone, in the Courts of Law, or in the Heads of Departments.

[3] The President shall have Power to fill up all Vacancies that may happen during the Recess of the Senate, by granting Commissions which shall expire at the End of their next Session.

Section 3. He shall from time to time give to the Congress Information of the State of the Union, and recommend to their Consideration such Measures as he shall judge necessary and expedient; he may, on extraordinary Occasions, convene both Houses, or either of them, and in Case of Disagreement between them, with Respect to the Time of Adjournment, he may adjourn them to such Time as he shall think proper; he shall receive Ambassadors and other public Ministers; he shall take Care that the Laws be faithfully executed, and shall Commission all the Officers of the United States.

Section 4. The President, Vice President and all civil Officers of the United States, shall be removed from Office on Impeachment for, and Conviction of, Treason, Bribery, or other high Crimes and Misdemeanors.

Article III

THE JUDICIAL BRANCH

Section 1. The judicial Power of the United States, shall be vested in one supreme Court, and in such inferior Courts as the Congress may from time to time ordain and establish. The Judges, both of the supreme and inferior Courts, shall hold their Offices during good Behaviour, and shall, at stated Times, receive for their Services, a Compensation, which shall not be diminished during their Continuance in Office.

Section 2. [1] The judicial Power shall extend to all Cases, in Law and Equity, arising under this Constitution, the Laws of the United States, and Treaties made, or which shall be made, under their Authority; —to all Cases affecting Ambassadors, other public Ministers and Consuls; —to all Cases of admiralty and maritime Jurisdiction; —to Controversies to which the United States shall be a Party; —to Controversies between two or more States, —[between a State and Citizens of another State;—] *(Note: Changed by the Eleventh Amendment.)* between Citizens of different States; —between Citizens of the same State claiming Lands under Grants of different States, [and between a State, or the Citizens thereof, and foreign States, Citizens or Subjects.] *(Note: Changed by the Eleventh Amendment.)*

[2] In all Cases affecting Ambassadors, other public Ministers and Consuls, and those in which a State shall be Party, the supreme Court shall have original Jurisdiction. In all the other Cases before mentioned, the supreme Court shall have appellate Jurisdiction, both as to Law and Fact, with such Exceptions, and under such Regulations as the Congress shall make.

[3] The Trial of all Crimes, except in Cases of Impeachment, shall be by Jury; and such Trial shall be held in the State where the said Crimes shall have been committed; but when not committed within any State, the Trial shall be at such Place or Places as the Congress may by Law have directed.

Section 3. [1] Treason against the United States, shall consist only in levying War against them, or in adhering to their Enemies, giving them Aid and Comfort. No Person shall be convicted of Treason unless on the Testimony of two Witnesses to the same overt Act, or on Confession in open Court.

[2] The Congress shall have Power to declare the Punishment of Treason, but no Attainder of Treason shall work Corruption of Blood, or Forfeiture except during the Life of the Person attainted.

Article IV

Section 1. Full Faith and Credit shall be given in each State to the public Acts, Records, and judicial Proceedings of every other State. And the Congress may by general Laws prescribe the Manner in which such Acts, Records and Proceedings shall be proved, and the Effect thereof.

Section 2. [1] The Citizens of each State shall be entitled to all Privileges and Immunities of Citizens in the several States.

[2] A Person charged in any State with Treason, Felony, or other Crime, who shall flee from Justice, and be found in another State, shall on demand of the executive Authority of the State from which he fled, be delivered up, to be removed to the State having Jurisdiction of the Crime.

[3] [No Person held to Service or Labour in one State, under the Laws thereof, escaping into another, shall, in Consequence of any Law or Regulation therein, be discharged from such Service or Labour, but shall be delivered up on Claim of the Party to whom such Service or Labour may be due.] *(Note: Superseded by the Thirteenth Amendment.)*

Section 3. [1] New States may be admitted by the Congress into this Union; but no new State shall be formed or erected within the Jurisdiction of any other State; nor any State be formed by the Junction of two or more States, or parts of States, without the Consent of the Legislatures of the States concerned as well as of the Congress.

[2] The Congress shall have Power to dispose of and make all needful Rules and Regulations respecting the Territory or other Property belonging to the United States; and nothing in this Constitution shall be so construed as to Prejudice any Claims of the United States, or of any particular State.

Section 4. The United States shall guarantee to every State in this Union a Republican Form of Government, and shall protect each of them against Invasion; and on Application of the Legislature, or of the Executive (when the Legislature cannot be convened) against domestic Violence.

Article V

The Congress, whenever two-thirds of both Houses shall deem it necessary, shall propose Amendments to this Constitution, or, on the Application of the Legislatures of two thirds of the several States, shall call a Convention for proposing Amendments, which, in either Case, shall be valid to all Intents and Purposes, as part of this Constitution, when ratified by the Legislatures of three-fourths of the several States, or by Conventions in three-fourths thereof, as the one or the other Mode of Ratification may be proposed by the Congress: Provided that no Amendment which may be made prior to the Year One thousand eight hundred and eight shall in any Manner affect the first and fourth Clauses in the Ninth Section of the first Article; and that no State, without its Consent, shall be deprived of its equal Suffrage in the Senate.

Article VI

NATIONAL DEBTS

[1] All Debts contracted and Engagements entered into, before the Adoption of this Constitution, shall be as valid against the United States under this Constitution, as under the Confederation.

SUPREMACY OF THE NATIONAL GOVERNMENT

[2] This Constitution, and the Laws of the United States which shall be made in Pursuance thereof; and all Treaties made, or which shall be made, under the Authority of the United States, shall be the supreme Law of the Land; and the Judges in every State shall be bound thereby, any Thing in the Constitution or Laws of any State to the Contrary notwithstanding.

[3] The Senators and Representatives before mentioned, and the Members of the several State Legislatures, and all executive and judicial Officers, both of the United States and of the several States, shall be bound by Oath or Affirmation, to support this Constitution; but no religious Test shall ever be required as a Qualification to any Office or public Trust under the United States.

Article VII

RATIFYING THE CONSTITUTION

The Ratification of the Conventions of nine States

shall be sufficient for the Establishment of this Constitution between the States so ratifying the Same.

Done in Convention by the Unanimous Consent of the States present the Seventeenth Day of September in the Year of our Lord one thousand seven hundred and Eighty seven and of the Independence of the United States of America the Twelfth.

In Witness whereof We have hereunto subscribed our Names.

George Washington—President
and deputy from Virginia

New Hampshire	John Langdon	Nicholas Gilman
Massachusetts	Nathaniel Gorham	Rufus King
Connecticut	Wm. Saml. Johnson	Roger Sherman
New York	Alexander Hamilton	
New Jersey	Wil: Livingston	David Brearley
	Wm. Paterson	Jona: Dayton
Pennsylvania	B. Franklin	Thomas Mifflin
	Robt Morris	Geo. Clymer
	T'hos. FitzSimons	Jared Ingersoll
	James Wilson	Gouv Morris
Delaware	Geo: Read	Gunning Bedford jun
	John Dickinson	Richard Basset
	Jaco: Broom	
Maryland	James McHenry	Dan of St Thos. Jenifer
	Danl Carroll	
Virginia	John Blair—	James Madison Jr.
North Carolina	Wm. Blount	Richd. Dobbs Spaight
	Hu Williamson	
South Carolina	J. Rutledge	Charles C. Pinckney
	Charles Pinckney	Pierce Butler
Georgia	William Few	Abr Baldwin

Attest William Jackson Secretary

AMENDMENTS TO THE CONSTITUTION

On September 25, 1789, Congress transmitted to the state legislatures twelve proposed amendments of which the first two dealt with Congressional representation and Congressional pay. Numbers three through twelve were adopted by the states to become the Bill of Rights in 1791. So, in effect amendment number three of the proposed twelve is our First Amendment. There is normally a seven-year time limit (with the possibility of an extension) for an amendment to be approved by three-fourths of the state legislatures (38 states) and to become a part of the Constitution. However, there were no time limitations set for the first twelve proposed amendments. Michigan became the thirty-eighth state to ratify the second proposed amendment that dealt with Congressional raises on May 7, 1992. Thus, two hundred and three years after it was introduced, the proposal placing restrictions on congressional pay raises became our twenty-seventh amendment and most immediate change to the Constitution.

THE BILL OF RIGHTS

The first ten Amendments (Bill of Rights) were ratified effective December 15, 1791.

AMENDMENT I

FREEDOM OF RELIGION, SPEECH, AND THE PRESS; RIGHTS OF ASSEMBLY AND PETITION

Congress shall make no law respecting an establishment of religion, or prohibiting the free exercise thereof; or abridging the freedom of speech, or of the press; or the right of the people peaceably to assemble, and to petition the Government for a redress of grievances.

AMENDMENT II

RIGHT TO BEAR ARMS

A well regulated Militia, being necessary to the security of a free State, the right of the people to keep and bear Arms, shall not be infringed.

AMENDMENT III
HOUSING OF SOLDIERS

No Soldier shall, in time of peace be quartered in any house, without the consent of the Owner, nor in time of war, but in a manner to be prescribed by law.

AMENDMENT IV
SEARCH AND ARREST WARRANTS

The right of the people to be secure in their persons, houses, papers, and effects, against unreasonable searches and seizures, shall not be violated, and no Warrants shall issue, but upon probable cause, supported by Oath or affirmation, and particularly describing the place to be searched, and the persons or things to be seized.

AMENDMENT V
RIGHTS IN CRIMINAL CASES

No person shall be held to answer for a capital, or otherwise infamous crime, unless on a presentment or indictment of a Grand Jury, except in cases arising in the land or naval forces, or in the Militia, when in actual service in time of War or public danger; nor shall any person be subject for the same offence to be twice put in jeopardy of life or limb; nor shall be compelled in any criminal case to be a witness against himself, nor be deprived of life, liberty, or property, without due process of law; nor shall private property be taken for public use, without just compensation.

AMENDMENT VI
RIGHTS TO A FAIR TRIAL

In all criminal prosecutions, the accused shall enjoy the right to a speedy and public trial, by an impartial jury of the State and district wherein the crime shall have been committed, which district shall have been previously ascertained by law, and to be informed of the nature and cause of the accusation; to be confronted with the witnesses against him; to have compulsory process for obtaining witnesses in his favor, and to have the Assistance of Counsel for his defence.

AMENDMENT VII
RIGHTS IN CIVIL CASES

In suits at common law, where the value in controversy shall exceed twenty dollars, the right of trial by jury shall be preserved, and no fact tried by a jury, shall be otherwise reexamined in any Court of the United States, than according to the rules of the common law.

AMENDMENT VIII
BAILS, FINES, AND PUNISHMENTS

Excessive bail shall not be required, nor excessive fines imposed, nor cruel and unusual punishments inflicted.

AMENDMENT IX
RIGHTS RETAINED BY THE PEOPLE

The enumeration in the Constitution, of certain rights, shall not be construed to deny or disparage others retained by the people.

AMENDMENT X
POWERS RETAINED BY THE STATES AND THE PEOPLE

The powers not delegated to the United States by the Constitution, nor prohibited by it to the States, are reserved to the States respectively, or to the people.

AMENDMENT XI
LAWSUITS AGAINST STATES

The Eleventh Amendment was proposed on March 4, 1794, and ratified on February 7, 1795. However, the amendment was not proclaimed until 1798 because of delays that occurred in certifying the ratification.

The Judicial power of the United States shall not be construed to extend to any suit in law or equity, commenced or prosecuted against one of the United States by Citizens of another State, or by Citizens or Subjects of any Foreign State.

AMENDMENT XII
ELECTION OF THE PRESIDENT AND VICE PRESIDENT

The Twelfth Amendment was proposed on December 9, 1803, and ratified on June 15, 1804.

The Electors shall meet in their respective states and vote by ballot for President and Vice-President, one of whom, at least, shall not be an inhabitant of the same state with themselves; they shall name in their ballots the person voted for as President, and in distinct ballots the person voted for as Vice-President, and they shall make distinct lists of all persons voted for as President, and of all persons voted for as Vice-President, and of the number of votes for each, which lists they shall sign and certify, and transmit sealed to the seat of the government of the United States, directed to the President of the Senate; —The President of the Senate shall, in presence of the Senate and House of Representatives, open all the certificates and the votes shall then be counted; —The person having the greatest number of votes for President, shall be the President, if such number be a majority of the whole number of Electors appointed; and if no person have such majority, then from the persons having the highest numbers not exceeding three on the list of those voted for as President, the House of Representatives shall choose immediately, by ballot, the President. But in choosing the President, the votes shall be taken by states, the representation from each state having one vote; a quorum for this purpose shall consist of a member or members from two-thirds of the states, and a majority of all the states shall be necessary to a choice. [And if the House of Representatives shall not choose a President whenever the right of choice shall devolve upon them, before the fourth day of March next following, then the Vice-President shall act as President, as in the case of the death or other constitutional disability of the President.] *(Note: Superseded by section 3 of the Twentieth Amendment.)* The person having the greatest of votes as Vice-President, shall be the Vice-President, if such number be a majority of the whole number of Electors appointed, and if no person have a majority, then from the two highest numbers on the list, the Senate shall choose the Vice-President; a quorum for the purpose shall consist of two-thirds of the whole number of Senators, and a majority of the whole number shall be necessary to a choice. But no person constitutionally ineligible to the office of President shall be eligible to that of Vice-President of the United States.

AMENDMENT XIII
ABOLITION OF SLAVERY

The Thirteenth Amendment was proposed on January 31, 1865, and ratified on December 6, 1865.

Section 1. Neither slavery nor involuntary servitude, except as a punishment for crime whereof the party shall have been duly convicted, shall exist within the United States, or any place subject to their jurisdiction.

Section 2. Congress shall have power to enforce this article by appropriate legislation.

AMENDMENT XIV
CIVIL RIGHTS

The Fourteenth Amendment was proposed on June 13, 1866, and ratified on July 9, 1868.

Section 1. All persons born or naturalized in the United States, and subject to the jurisdiction thereof, are citizens of the United States and of the State wherein they reside. No State shall make or enforce any law which shall abridge the privileges or immunities of citizens of the United States; nor shall any State deprive any person of life, liberty, or property, without due process of law; nor deny to any person within its jurisdiction the equal protection of the laws.

Section 2. Representatives shall be apportioned among the several States according to their respective numbers, counting the whole number of persons in each State, excluding Indians not taxed. But when the right to vote at any election for the choice of electors for President and Vice-President of the United States, Representatives in Congress, the Executive and Judicial officers of a State, or the members of the Legislature thereof, is denied to any of the male inhabitants of such State, being twenty-one years of age, *(Note: Changed by section 1 of the Twenty-Sixth Amendment.)* and citizens of the United States, or in any way abridged, except for participation in rebellion, or other crime, the basis of representation therein shall be reduced in the proportion which the number of such male citizens shall bear to the whole number of male citizens twenty-one years of age in such State.

Section 3. No person shall be a Senator or Representative in Congress, or elector of President and Vice-President, or hold any office, civil or military, under the United States, or under any State, who, having previously taken an oath, as a member of Congress, or as an officer of the United States, or as a member of any State legislature, or as an executive or judicial officer of any State, to support the Constitution of the United States, shall have engaged in insurrection or rebellion against the same, or given aid or comfort to the enemies thereof. But Congress may by a vote of two-thirds of each House, remove such disability.

Section 4. The validity of the public debt of the United States, authorized by law, including debts incurred for payment of pensions and bounties for services in suppressing insurrection or rebellion, shall not be questioned. But neither the United States nor any State shall assume or pay any debt or obligation incurred in aid of insurrection or rebellion against the United States, or any claim for the loss or emancipation of any slave; but all such debts, obligations and claims shall be held illegal and void.

Section 5. The Congress shall have power to enforce, by appropriate legislation, the provisions of this article.

AMENDMENT XV
BLACK SUFFRAGE

The Fifteenth Amendment was proposed on February 26, 1869, and ratified on February 3, 1870.

Section 1. The right of citizens of the United States to vote shall not be denied or abridged by the United States or by any State on account of race, color, or previous condition of servitude—

Section 2. The Congress shall have power to enforce this article by appropriate legislation.

AMENDMENT XVI
INCOME TAXES

The Sixteenth Amendment was proposed on July 12, 1909, and ratified on February 3, 1913.

The Congress shall have power to lay and collect taxes on incomes, from whatever source derived, without apportionment among the several States, and without regard to any census or enumeration.

AMENDMENT XVII
DIRECT ELECTION OF SENATORS

The Seventeenth Amendment was proposed on May 13, 1912, and ratified on April 8, 1913.

The Senate of the United States shall be composed of two Senators from each State, elected by the people thereof, for six years; and each Senator shall have one vote. The electors in each State shall have the qualifications requisite for electors of the most numerous branch of the State legislatures.

When vacancies happen in the representation of any State in the Senate, the executive authority of such State shall issue writs of election to fill such vacancies: *Provided,* That the legislature of any State may empower the executive thereof to make temporary appointments: until the people fill the vacancies by election as the legislature may direct.

This amendment shall not be so construed as to affect the election or term of any Senator chosen before it becomes valid as part of the Constitution.

AMENDMENT XVIII
PROHIBITION OF LIQUOR

The Eighteenth Amendment was proposed on December 18, 1917, and ratified on January 16, 1919. It was repealed by the Twenty-First Amendment on December 5, 1933.

[**Section 1**. After one year from the ratification of this article the manufacture, sale, or transportation of intoxicating liquors within, the importation thereof into, or the exportation thereof from the United States and all territory subject to the jurisdiction thereof for beverage purposes is hereby prohibited.

Section 2. The Congress and the several States shall have concurrent power to enforce this article by appropriate legislation.

Section 3. This article shall be inoperative unless it shall have been ratified as an amendment to the Constitution by the legislatures of the several States as provided in the Constitution, within seven years from the date of the submission hereof to the States by the Congress.]

AMENDMENT XIX
WOMAN SUFFRAGE

The Nineteenth Amendment was proposed on June 4, 1919, and ratified on August 18, 1920.

The right of citizens of the United States to vote shall not be denied or abridged by the United States or by any State on account of sex.

Congress shall have power to enforce this article by appropriate legislation.

AMENDMENT XX
TERMS OF THE PRESIDENT AND CONGRESS

The Twentieth Amendment was proposed on March 2, 1932, and ratified on January 23, 1933.

Section 1. The terms of the President and Vice President shall end at noon on the 20th day of January, and the terms of Senators and Representatives at noon on the 3d day of January, of the years in which such terms would have ended if this article had not been ratified; and the terms of their successors shall then begin.

Section 2. The Congress shall assemble at least once in every year, and such meeting shall begin at noon on the 3d day of January, unless they shall by law appoint a different day.

Section 3. If, at the time fixed for the beginning of the term of the President, the President elect shall have died, the Vice President elect shall become President. If a President shall not have been chosen before the time fixed for the beginning of his term, or if the President elect shall have failed to qualify, then the Vice President elect shall act as President until a President shall have qualified; and the Congress may by law provide for the case wherein neither a President elect nor a Vice President elect shall have qualified, declaring who shall then act as President, or the manner in which one who is to act shall be selected, and such person shall act accordingly until a President or Vice President shall have qualified.

Section 4. The Congress may by law provide for the case of the death of any of the persons from whom the House of Representatives may choose a President whenever the right of choice shall have devolved upon them, and for the case of the death of any of the persons from whom the Senate may choose a Vice President whenever the right of choice shall have devolved upon them.

Section 5. Sections 1 and 2 shall take effect on the 15th day of October following the ratification of this article.

Section 6. This article shall be inoperative unless it shall have been ratified as an amendment to the Constitution by the legislatures of three-fourths of the several States within seven years from the date of its submission.

AMENDMENT XXI
REPEAL OF PROHIBITION

The Twenty-First Amendment was proposed on February 20, 1933, and ratified on December 5, 1933.

Section 1. The eighteenth article of amendment to the Constitution of the United States is hereby repealed.

Section 2. The transportation or importation into any State, Territory, or possession of the United States for delivery or use therein of intoxicating liquors, in violation of the laws thereof, is hereby prohibited.

Section 3. This article shall be inoperative unless it shall have been ratified as an amendment to the Constitution by conventions in the several States, as provided in the Constitution, within seven years from the date of the submission hereof to the States by the Congress.

AMENDMENT XXII
LIMITATION OF PRESIDENTS TO TWO TERMS

The Twenty-Second Amendment was proposed on March 24, 1947, and ratified on February 27, 1951.

Section 1. No person shall be elected to the office of the President more than twice, and no person who has held the office of President, or acted as President, for more than two years of a term to which some other person was elected President shall be elected to the office of the President more than once. But this Article shall not apply to any person holding the office of President when this Article was proposed by the Congress, and shall not prevent any person who may be holding the office of President, or acting as President, during the term within which this Article becomes operative from holding the office of President or acting as President during the remainder of such term.

Section 2. This article shall be inoperative unless it shall have been ratified as an amendment to the Constitution by the legislatures of three-fourths of the several States within seven years from the date of its submission to the States by the Congress.

AMENDMENT XXIII
SUFFRAGE IN THE DISTRICT OF COLUMBIA
The Twenty-Third Amendment was proposed on June 16, 1960, and ratified on March 29, 1961.

Section 1. The District constituting the seat of Government of the United States shall appoint in such manner as the Congress may direct:

A number of electors of President and Vice President equal to the whole number of Senators and Representatives in Congress to which the District would be entitled if it were a State, but in no event more than the least populous State; they shall be in addition to those appointed by the States, but they shall be considered, for the purposes of the election of President and Vice President, to be electors appointed by a State; and they shall meet in the District and perform such duties as provided by the twelfth article of amendment.

Section 2. The Congress shall have power to enforce this article by appropriate legislation.

AMENDMENT XXIV
POLL TAXES
The Twenty-Fourth Amendment was proposed on August 27, 1962, and ratified on January 23, 1964.

Section 1. The right of citizens of the United States to vote in any primary or other election for President or Vice President, for electors for President or Vice President, or for Senator or Representative in Congress, shall not be denied or abridged by the United States or any State by reason of failure to pay any poll tax or other tax.

Section 2. The Congress shall have power to enforce this article by appropriate legislation.

AMENDMENT XXV

PRESIDENTIAL DISABILITY AND SUCCESSION

The Twenty-Fifth Amendment was proposed on July 6, 1965, and ratified on February 10, 1967.

Section 1. In case of the removal of the President from office or of his death or resignation, the Vice President shall become President.

Section 2. Whenever there is a vacancy in the office of the Vice President, the President shall nominate a Vice President who shall take office upon confirmation by a majority vote of both Houses of Congress.

Section 3. Whenever the President transmits to the President pro tempore of the Senate and the Speaker of the House of Representatives his written declaration that he is unable to discharge the powers and duties of his office, and until he transmits to them a written declaration to the contrary, such powers and duties shall be discharged by the Vice President as Acting President.

Section 4. Whenever the Vice President and a majority of either the principal officers of the executive departments or of such other body as Congress may by law provide, transmit to the President pro tempore of the Senate and the Speaker of the House of Representatives their written declaration that the President is unable to discharge the powers and duties of his office, the Vice President shall immediately assume the powers and duties of the office as Acting President.

Thereafter, when the President transmits to the President pro tempore of the Senate and the Speaker of the House of Representatives his written declaration that no inability exists, he shall resume the powers and duties of his office unless the Vice President and a majority of either the principal officers of the executive department or of such other body as Congress may by law provide, transmit within four days to the President pro tempore of the Senate and the Speaker of the House of Representatives their written declaration that the President is unable to discharge the powers and duties of his office. Thereupon Congress shall decide the issue, assembling within forty-eight hours for that purpose if not in session. If the Congress, within twenty-one days after receipt of the latter written declaration, or, if Congress is not in session, within twenty-one days after Congress is required to assemble, determines by two-thirds vote of both Houses that the President is unable to discharge the powers and duties of his office, the Vice President shall continue to discharge the same as Acting President; otherwise, the President shall resume the powers and duties of his office.

AMENDMENT XXVI
SUFFRAGE FOR EIGHTEEN-YEAR-OLDS

The Twenty-Sixth Amendment was proposed on March 23, 1971, and ratified on July 1, 1971.

Section 1. The right of citizens of the United States, who are eighteen years of age or older, to vote shall not be denied or abridged by the United States or by any State on account of age.

Section 2. The Congress shall have power to enforce this article by appropriate legislation.

AMENDMENT XXVII
CONGRESSIONAL SALARIES

The Twenty-Seventh Amendment was proposed on September 25, 1789, and ratified on May 7, 1992.

No Law, varying the compensation for the services of the Senators and Representatives, shall take effect, until an election of Representatives shall have intervened.

Only one amendment has overturned a previous amendment. The Twenty-First Amendment (1933) repealed the prohibition of alcohol, which was established by the Eighteenth Amendment (1919).

AMENDMENTS PROPOSED BUT NEVER RATIFIED

One of the enduring features of our Constitution is its flexibility. At the time of its ratification, the population of the United States was around 4 million. Today that population exceeds 315 million. From the time of its adoption, the Constitution has only changed 27 times! Actually, since 1791 (with the inclusion of the Bill of Rights) it has only changed 17 times—extraordinary, in light of radical shifts in technology, infrastructure, population, and other changes that have occurred in this country during the last 200 some years.

The framers of the Constitution realized that no document could cover all of the changes that would take place in the future. To ensure its longevity, they developed procedures for amending it. In order for an amendment to be passed, a number of steps must be taken as outlined in Article V of the Constitution. The article provides two methods for the proposal and two methods for the ratification of an amendment. An amendment may be proposed by a two-thirds vote of the House of Representatives and the Senate or a national convention called by Congress at the request of two-thirds of the state legislatures. The latter procedure has never been used. The amendment may then be ratified by three-fourths of the state legislatures (38 states) or special conventions called by three-fourths of the states. The Twenty-First amendment was the only one to be adopted in this way. However, it is within the power of Congress to decide which method of ratification will be used.

The time limit for the ratification process of seven years was first applied to the Eighteenth Amendment. There have been more than 10,000 amendments proposed in Congress since 1789, and fewer than one percent of them have received enough support to actually go through the constitutional ratification process.

The following is a very limited list of some of the proposed amendments that never left the halls of Congress:

1876 An attempt to abolish the United States Senate

1876 The forbidding of religious leaders from occupying a governmental office or receiving federal funding

1878 An Executive Council of Three to replace the office of President

1893 Renaming this nation the "United States of the Earth"

1893 Abolishing the United States Army and Navy

1894 Acknowledging that the Constitution recognize God and Jesus Christ as the supreme authorities in human affairs

1912 Making marriage between races illegal

1914 Finding divorce to be illegal

1916 All acts of war should be put to a national vote. Anyone voting yes had to register as a volunteer for service in the United States Army.

1933 An attempt to limit personal wealth to $1 million

1936 An attempt to allow the American people to vote on whether or not the United States should go to war

1938 The forbidding of drunkenness in the United States and all of its territories

1947 The income tax maximum for an individual should not exceed 25%

1948 The right of citizens to segregate themselves from others

1971 American citizens should have the alienable right to an environment free of pollution

THE DECLARATION OF INDEPENDENCE

IN CONGRESS, July 4, 1776.
The unanimous Declaration of the thirteen united
States of America,

WHEN in the Course of human Events, it becomes necessary for one People to dissolve the Political Bands which have connected them with another, and to assume among the Powers of the Earth, the separate and equal Station to which the Laws of Nature and of Nature's God entitle them, a decent Respect to the Opinions of Mankind requires that they should declare the causes which impel them to the Separation.

WE hold these Truths to be self-evident, that all Men are created equal, that they are endowed by their Creator with certain unalienable Rights, that among these are Life, Liberty, and the Pursuit of Happiness—That to secure these Rights, Governments are instituted among Men, deriving their just Powers from the Consent of the Governed, that whenever any Form of Government becomes destructive of these Ends, it is the Right of the People to alter or to abolish it, and to institute new Government, laying its Foundation on such Principles, and organizing its Powers in such Form, as to them shall seem most likely to effect their Safety and Happiness. Prudence, indeed, will dictate that Governments long established should not be changed for light and transient Causes; and accordingly all Experience hath shewn, that Mankind are more disposed to suffer, while Evils are sufferable, than to right themselves by abolishing the Forms to which they are accustomed. But when a long Train of Abuses and Usurpations, pursuing invariably the same Object, evinces a Design to reduce them under absolute Despotism, it is their Right, it is their Duty, to throw off such Government, and to provide new Guards for their future Security. Such has been the patient Sufferance of these Colonies; and such is now the Necessity which constrains them to alter their former Systems of Government. The History of the present King of Great-Britain is a History of repeated Injuries and Usurpations, all having in direct Object the Establishment of an absolute Tyranny over these States. To prove this, let Facts be submitted to a candid World.

He has refused his Assent to Laws, the most wholesome and necessary for the public Good.

He has forbidden his Governors to pass Laws of immediate and pressing Importance, unless suspended in their Operation till his Assent should be obtained; and when so suspended, he has utterly neglected to attend to them.

He has refused to pass other Laws for the Accommodation of large Districts of People, unless those People would relinquish the Right of Representation in the Legislature, a Right inestimable to them, and formidable to Tyrants only.

He has called together Legislative Bodies at Places unusual, uncomfortable, and distant from the Depository of their public Records, for the sole Purpose of fatiguing them into Compliance with his Measures.

He has dissolved Representative Houses repeatedly, for opposing with manly Firmness his Invasions on the Rights of the People.

He has refused for a long Time, after such Dissolutions, to cause others to be elected; whereby the Legislative Powers, incapable of Annihilation, have returned to the People at large for their exercise; the State remaining in the mean time exposed to all the Dangers of Invasion from without, and Convulsions within.

He has endeavoured to prevent the Population of these States; for that Purpose obstructing the Laws for Naturalization of Foreigners; refusing to pass others to encourage their Migrations hither, and raising the Conditions of new Appropriations of Lands.

He has obstructed the Administration of Justice, by refusing his assent to Laws for establishing Judiciary Powers.

He has made Judges dependent on his Will alone, for the Tenure of their Offices, and the Amount and Payment of their Salaries.

He has erected a Multitude of new Offices, and sent hither Swarms of Officers to harrass our People, and eat out their Substance.

He has kept among us, in Times of Peace, Standing Armies, without the consent of our Legislatures.

He has affected to render the Military independent of and superior to the Civil Power.

He has combined with others to subject us to a Jurisdiction foreign to our Constitution, and unacknowledged by our Laws; giving his Assent to their Acts of pretended Legislation:

For quartering large Bodies of Armed Troops among us:

For protecting them, by a mock Trial, from Punishment for any Murders which they should commit on the Inhabitants of these States:

For cutting off our Trade with all Parts of the World:

For imposing Taxes on us without our Consent:

For depriving us, in many Cases, of the Benefits of Trial by Jury:

For transporting us beyond Seas to be tried for pretended Offences:

For abolishing the free System of English Laws in a neighbouring Province, establishing therein an arbitrary Government and enlarging its Boundaries, so as to render it at once an Example and fit Instrument for introducing the same absolute Rule into these Colonies:

For taking away our Charters, abolishing our most valuable Laws, and altering fundamentally the Forms of our Governments:

For suspending our own Legislatures, and declaring themselves invested with Power to legislate for us in all Cases whatsoever.

He has abdicated Government here, by declaring us out of his Protection and waging War against us.

He has plundered our Seas, ravaged our Coasts, burnt our Towns, and destroyed the Lives of our People.

He is, at this Time, transporting large Armies of foreign Mercenaries to compleat the Works of Death, Desolation, and Tyranny already begun with circumstances of Cruelty and Perfidy, scarcely paralleled in the most barbarous Ages, and totally unworthy of the Head of a civilized Nation.

He has constrained our fellow Citizens taken Captive on the high Seas to bear Arms against their Country, to become the Executioners of their friends and Brethren, or to fall themselves by their Hands.

He has excited domestic Insurrections amongst us, and has endeavoured to bring on the Inhabitants of our Frontiers, the merciless Indian Savages, whose known Rule of Warfare, is an undistinguished Destruction of all Ages, Sexes and Conditions.

In every stage of these Oppressions we have Petitioned for Redress in the most humble Terms: Our repeated Petitions have been answered only by repeated Injury. A Prince, whose Character is thus marked by every act which may define a Tyrant, is unfit to be the Ruler of a free People.

Nor have we been wanting in Attentions to our British Brethren. We have warned them from Time to Time of Attempts by their Legislature to extend an unwarrantable jurisdiction over us. We have reminded them of the Circumstances of our Emigration and Settlement here. We have appealed to their native justice and Magnanimity, and we have conjured them by the Ties of our common Kindred to disavow these Usurpations, which, would inevitably interrupt our Connections and Correspondence. They too have been deaf to the Voice of Justice and of Consanguinity. We must, therefore, acquiesce in the Necessity, which denounces our Separation, and hold them, as we hold the rest of Mankind, Enemies in War, in Peace, Friends.

We, therefore, the Representatives of the UNITED STATES OF AMERICA, in General Congress, Assembled, appealing to the Supreme Judge of the World for the Rectitude of our Intentions, do, in the Name, and by Authority of the good People of these Colonies, solemnly Publish and Declare, That these United Colonies are, and of Right ought to be, FREE AND INDEPENDENT STATES, that they are absolved from all Allegiance to the

British Crown, and that all political Connection between them and the State of Great-Britain, is and ought to be totally dissolved; and that as FREE AND INDEPENDENT STATES, they have full Power to levy War, conclude Peace, contract Alliances, establish Commerce, and to do all other Acts and Things which INDEPENDENT STATES may of right do. And for the support of this Declaration, with a firm Reliance on the Protection of divine Providence, we mutually pledge to each other our Lives, our Fortunes, and our sacred Honor.

> *"A free government is a complicated piece of machinery, the nice and exact adjustment of whose springs, wheels, and weights, is not yet well comprehended by the artists of the age, and still less by the people."*
> —JOHN ADAMS
> TO THOMAS JEFFERSON
> MAY 19, 1821

> *"Don't interfere with anything in the Constitution. That must be maintained, for it is the only safeguard of our liberties."*
> —ABRAHAM LINCOLN

> *"In free countries, every man is entitled to express his opinions and every other man is entitled not to listen."*
> —G. NORMAN COLLIE

> *"The happy Union of these States is a wonder; their Constitution a miracle; their example the hope of Liberty throughout the world."*
> —JAMES MADISON

DATES TO REMEMBER
(The Articles of Confederation)

March 1, 1781: The state of Maryland officially ratifies the Articles of Confederation, and the document is declared "in force." The following day Congress takes the name "The United States in Congress Assembled."

June 20, 1782: The Great Seal of the United States is officially adopted by the Congress of the Confederation.

January 11, 1785: Congress moves to New York City which becomes the temporary capital of the United States of America.

May 8, 1785: Congress passes the Land Ordinance of 1785 that deals with a systematic and orderly procedure to settle the areas of the Northwest Territory.

September 11-14, 1786: A meeting is convened in Annapolis, Maryland, to discuss the economic instability of the country under the Articles of Confederation. Only five states come to the meeting, but there is a call for another meeting to take place in Philadelphia the following year with the express purpose of revising the Articles of Confederation.

September 26, 1786: A rebellion begins in Massachusetts led by Daniel Shays, a former captain in the Revolutionary War. The issue is the unstable economic condition of the farmers in the western part of the state.

February 4, 1787: A militia raised by the state of Massachusetts is instrumental in ending Shays' Rebellion. Although the rebellion is unsuccessful, there is a call in the state to avoid direct taxation, lower court costs, and provide some exemptions to the debt process. The rebellion also alarms the conservative patriots in the country and helps in calling for a stronger federal constitution.

February 21, 1787: Congress gives official approval of the meeting to take place in Philadelphia on May 14, 1787, to revise the Articles of Confederation.

AN INTRODUCTION TO THE ARTICLES OF CONFEDERATION
America's First Constitution

The first constitution in our nation's history was the Articles of Confederation. Under the Articles of Confederation we took "baby steps" as a nation. The government conducted the affairs of the country during the last two years of the Revolutionary War, helped to negotiate the Treaty of Paris in 1783, and produced two monumental pieces of legislation in the Land Ordinance of 1785 and the Northwest Ordinance of 1787.

While the Articles of Confederation was a plan of government based upon the principles fought for in the American Revolutionary War, it contained crucial flaws. It had no power of national taxation, no power to control trade, and it provided for a comparatively weak executive. Therefore, it could not enforce legislation. It was a "league of friendship" which was opposed to any type of national authority. The Articles of Confederation's greatest weakness, however, was that it had no direct origin in the people themselves—it knew only state sovereignty. Each state, therefore, had the power to collect its own taxes, issue currency, and provide for its own militia. The government could not govern effectively because of a general lack of power to compel states to honor national obligations. The government's main activity was to control foreign policy and conclude treaties. Economic credibility was a major problem because the government owed $42 million (more than $42 billion today) after the Revolutionary War, and the debt was mainly owed to American patriots. This financial obligation was not paid off until the early part of the 1800's.

It would have been very difficult for our country to have created a stronger second constitution without learning from the mistakes of the first. The Articles of Confederation served as a "transition" between the Revolutionary War and the Constitution.

JOHN HANSON
America's First President

When we think of the President of the United States, many people do not realize that we are actually referring to presidents elected under the U.S. Constitution. Everybody knows that the first president in that sense was George Washington. But in fact the Articles of Confederation, the predecessor to the Constitution, also called for a president—albeit one with greatly diminished powers. Eight men were appointed to serve one-year terms as president under the Articles of Confederation. The first of these was John Hanson, in 1781. His exact title was the "President of the United States in Congress Assembled."

The Articles of Confederation did not specifically "define" the powers of the President, and so under Hanson's leadership various departments of the government were formed. He alone had the authority to correspond and negotiate with foreign governments. During his year in office, he approved the Great Seal of the United States that is still used today and helped establish the first U.S. Treasury Department. He led the fight to guarantee the statehood of the Western Territories beyond the Appalachian Mountains that had been controlled by some of the original thirteen colonies.

Upon his death on November 21, 1783, the following eulogy appeared in the *Maryland Gazette*:

"Thus was ended the career of one of America's greatest statesmen. While hitherto practically unknown to our people, and this is true as to nearly all the generations that have lived since his day, his great handiwork, the nation which he helped to establish, remains as a fitting tribute to his memory. It is doubtful if there has ever lived on this side of the Atlantic, a nobler character or shrewder statesman. One would search in vain to find a more powerful personage, or a more aggressive leader, in the annals of American history. And it is extremely doubtful if there has ever lived in an age since the advent of civilization, a man with a keener grasp of, or a deeper insight into, such democratic ideals as are essential to the promotion of personal liberty and the extension of human happiness. He was firm in his opinion that the people of America were capable of ruling themselves without the aid of a king."

THE ARTICLES OF CONFEDERATION

To all to whom these Presents shall come, we the under-signed Delegates of the States affixed to our Names send greeting.

The Articles of Confederation and Perpetual Union Between The States Of New Hampshire, Massachusetts-bay Rhode Island and Providence Plantations, Connecticut, New York, New Jersey, Pennsylvania, Delaware, Maryland, Virginia, North Carolina, South Carolina and Georgia.

Article I

The Stile of this Confederacy shall be "The United States of America".

Article II

Each state retains its sovereignty, freedom, and independence, and every power, jurisdiction, and right, which is not by this Confederation expressly delegated to the United States, in Congress assembled.

Article III

The said States hereby severally enter into a firm league of friendship with each other, for their common defense, the security of their liberties, and their mutual and general welfare, binding themselves to assist each other, against all force offered to, or attacks made upon them, or any of them, on account of religion, sovereignty, trade, or any other pretense whatever.

Article IV

The better to secure and perpetuate mutual friendship and intercourse among the people of the different States in this Union, the free inhabitants of each of these States, paupers, vagabonds, and fugitives from justice excepted, shall be entitled to all privileges and immunities of free citizens in the several States; and the people of each State shall free ingress and regress to and from any other State, and shall enjoy therein all the privileges of trade and commerce, subject to the same duties, impositions, and restrictions as the inhabitants thereof respectively, provided that such restrictions shall not extend so far as to prevent the removal of property imported into any State, to any other State, of which the owner is an inhabitant; provided also that no imposition, duties or restriction shall be laid by any State, on the property of the United States, or either of them.

If any person guilty of, or charged with, treason, felony, or other high misdemeanor in any State, shall flee from justice, and be found in any of the United States, he shall, upon demand of the Governor or executive power of the State from which he fled, be delivered up and removed to the State having jurisdiction of his offense.

Full faith and credit shall be given in each of these States to the records, acts, and judicial proceedings of the courts and magistrates of every other State.

Article V

For the most convenient management of the general interests of the United States, delegates shall be annually appointed in such manner as the legislatures of each State shall direct, to meet in Congress on the first Monday in November, in every year, with a power reserved to each State to recall its delegates, or any of them, at any time within the year, and to send others in their stead for the remainder of the year.

No State shall be represented in Congress by less than two, nor more than seven members; and no person shall be capable of being a delegate for more than three years in any term of six years; nor shall any person, being a delegate, be capable of holding any office under the United States, for which he, or another for his benefit, receives any salary, fees or emolument of any kind.

Each State shall maintain its own delegates in a meeting of the States, and while they act as members of the committee of the States.

In determining questions in the United States in Congress assembled, each State shall have one vote.

Freedom of speech and debate in Congress shall not be impeached or questioned in any court or place out of Congress, and the members of Congress shall be protected in their persons from arrests or imprisonments, during the time of their going to and from, and attendence on Congress, except for treason, felony, or breach of the peace.

Article VI

No State, without the consent of the United States in Congress assembled, shall send any embassy to, or receive any embassy from, or enter into any conference, agreement, alliance or treaty with any King, Prince or State; nor shall any person holding any office of profit or trust under the United States, or any of them, accept any present, emolument, office or title of any kind whatever from any King, Prince or foreign State; nor shall the United States in Congress assembled, or any of them, grant any title of nobility.

No two or more States shall enter into any treaty, confederation or alliance whatever between them, without the consent of the United States in Congress assembled, specifying accurately the purposes for which the same is to be entered into, and how long it shall continue.

No State shall lay any imposts or duties, which may interfere with any stipulations in treaties, entered into by the United States in Congress assembled, with any King, Prince or State, in pursuance of any treaties already proposed by Congress, to the courts of France and Spain.

No vessel of war shall be kept up in time of peace by any State, except such number only, as shall be deemed necessary by the United States in Congress assembled, for the defense of such State, or its trade; nor shall any body of forces be kept up by any State in time of peace, except such number only, as in the judgement of the United States in Congress assembled, shall be deemed requisite to garrison the forts necessary for the defense of such State; but every State shall always keep up a well-regulated and disciplined militia, sufficiently armed and accoutered, and shall provide and constantly have ready for use, in public stores, a due number of filed pieces and tents, and a proper quantity of arms, ammunition and camp equipage.

No State shall engage in any war without the consent of the United States in Congress assembled, unless such

State be actually invaded by enemies, or shall have received certain advice of a resolution being formed by some nation of Indians to invade such State, and the danger is so imminent as not to admit of a delay till the United States in Congress assembled can be consulted; nor shall any State grant commissions to any ships or vessels of war, nor letters of marque or reprisal, except it be after a declaration of war by the United States in Congress assembled, and then only against the Kingdom or State and the subjects thereof, against which war has been so declared, and under such regulations as shall be established by the United States in Congress assembled, unless such State be infested by pirates, in which case vessels of war may be fitted out for that occasion, and kept so long as the danger shall continue, or until the United States in Congress assembled shall determine otherwise.

Article VII

When land forces are raised by any State for the common defense, all officers of or under the rank of colonel, shall be appointed by the legislature of each State respectively, by whom such forces shall be raised, or in such manner as such State shall direct, and all vacancies shall be filled up by the State which first made the appointment.

Article VIII

All charges of war, and all other expenses that shall be incurred for the common defense or general welfare, and allowed by the United States in Congress assembled, shall be defrayed out of a common treasury, which shall be supplied by the several States in proportion to the value of all land within each State, granted or surveyed for any person, as such land and the buildings and improvements thereon shall be estimated according to such mode as the United States in Congress assembled, shall from time to time direct and appoint.

The taxes for paying that proportion shall be laid and levied by the authority and direction of the legislatures of the several States within the time agreed upon by the United States in Congress assembled.

Article IX

The United States in Congress assembled, shall have the sole and exclusive right and power of determining on peace and war, except in the cases mentioned in the sixth article—of sending and receiving ambassadors—entering into treaties and alliances, provided that no treaty of commerce shall be made whereby the legislative power of the respective States shall be restrained from imposing such imposts and duties on foreigners, as their own people are subjected to, or from prohibiting the exportation or importation of any species of goods or commodities whatsoever—of establishing rules for deciding in all cases, what captures on land or water shall be legal, and in what manner prizes taken by land or naval forces in the service of the United States shall be divided or appropriated—of granting letters of marque and reprisal in times of peace—appointing courts for the trial of piracies and felonies commited on the high seas and establishing courts for receiving and determining finally appeals in all cases of captures, provided that no member of Congress shall be appointed a judge of any of the said courts.

The United States in Congress assembled shall also be the last resort on appeal in all disputes and differences now subsisting or that hereafter may arise between two or more States concerning boundary, jurisdiction or any other causes whatever; which authority shall always be exercised in the manner following. Whenever the legislative or executive authority or lawful agent of any State in controversy with another shall present a petition to Congress stating the matter in question and praying for a hearing, notice thereof shall be given by order of Congress to the legislative or executive authority of the other State in controversy, and a day assigned for the appearance of the parties by their lawful agents, who shall then be directed to appoint by joint consent, commissioners or judges to constitute a court for hearing and determining the matter in question: but if they cannot agree, Congress shall name three persons out of each of the United States, and from the list of such persons each party shall alternately strike out one, the petitioners beginning, until the number shall be reduced to thirteen; and from that number not less than seven, nor more than nine names as Congress shall direct, shall in the presence of Congress be drawn out by lot, and the persons whose names shall be so drawn or any five of them, shall be commissioners or judges, to hear and finally determine the controversy, so always as a major part of the judges who shall hear the cause shall agree in the determination: and if either party shall neglect to attend at the day appointed, without showing reasons, which Congress shall judge sufficient, or being present shall refuse to strike, the Congress shall proceed to nominate three persons out of each State, and the secretary of Congress shall strike in behalf of such party absent or refusing; and the judgement and sentence of the court to be appointed, in the manner before prescribed, shall be final and conclusive; and if any of the parties shall refuse to submit to the authority of such court, or to appear or defend their claim or cause, the court shall nevertheless proceed to pronounce sentence, or judgement, which shall in like manner be final and decisive, the judgement or sentence and other proceedings being in either case transmitted to Congress, and lodged among the acts of Congress for the security of the parties concerned: provided that every commissioner, before he sits in judgement, shall take an oath to be administered by one of the judges of the supreme or superior court of the State, where the cause shall be tried, 'well and truly to hear and determine the matter in question, according to the best of his judgement, without favor, affection or hope of reward': provided also, that no State shall be deprived of territory for the benefit of the United States.

All controversies concerning the private right of soil claimed under different grants of two or more States, whose jurisdictions as they may respect such lands, and the States which passed such grants are adjusted, the said grants or either of them being at the same time claimed to have originated antecedent to such settlement of jurisdiction, shall on the petition of either party to the Congress of the United States, be finally determined as near as may be in the same manner as is before prescribed for deciding disputes respecting territorial jurisdiction between different States.

The United States in Congress assembled shall also have the sole and exclusive right and power of regulating the alloy and value of coin struck by their own authority, or by that of the respective States—fixing the standards of weights and measures throughout the United States—regulating the trade and managing all affairs with the Indians, not members of any of the States, provided that the legislative right of any State within its own limits be not infringed or violated—establishing or regulating post offices from one State to another, throughout all the United States, and exacting such postage on the papers passing through the same as may be requisite to defray the expenses of the said office—appointing all officers of the land forces, in the service of the United States, excepting regimental officers—appointing all the officers of the naval forces, and commissioning all officers whatever in the service of the United States—making rules for the government and regulation of the said land and naval forces, and directing their operations.

The United States in Congress assembled shall have authority to appoint a committee, to sit in the recess of Congress, to be denominated 'A Committee of the States', and to consist of one delegate from each State; and to appoint such other committees and civil officers as may be necessary for managing the general affairs of the United States under their direction—to appoint one of their members to preside, provided that no person be allowed to serve in the office of president more than one year in any term of three years; to ascertain the necessary sums of money to be raised for the service of the United States, and to appropriate and apply the same for defraying the public expenses—to borrow money, or emit bills on the credit of the United States, transmitting every half-year to the respective States an account of the sums of money so borrowed or emitted—to build and equip a navy—to agree upon the number of land forces, and to make requisitions from each State for its quota, in proportion to the number of white inhabitants in such State; which requisition shall be binding, and thereupon the legislature of each State shall appoint the regimental officers, raise the men and cloath, arm and equip them in a solid-like manner, at the expense of the United States; and the officers and men so cloathed, armed and equipped shall march to the place appointed, and within the time agreed on by the United States in Congress assembled. But if the United States in Congress assembled shall, on consideration of circumstances judge proper that any State should not raise men, or should raise a smaller number of men than the quota thereof, such extra number shall be raised, officered, cloathed, armed and equipped in the same manner as the quota of each State, unless the legislature of such State shall judge that such extra number cannot be safely spread out in the same, in which case they shall raise, officer, cloath, arm and equip as many of such extra number as they judge can be safely spared. And the officers and men so cloathed, armed, and equipped, shall march to the place appointed, and within the time agreed on by the United States in Congress assembled.

The United States in Congress assembled shall never engage in a war, nor grant letters of marque or reprisal in time of peace, nor enter into any treaties or alliances, nor coin money, nor regulate the value thereof, nor ascertain the sums and expenses necessary for the defense and welfare of the United States, or any of them, nor emit bills, nor borrow money on the credit of the United States, nor appropriate money, nor agree upon the number of vessels of war, to be built or purchased, or the number of land or sea forces to be raised, nor appoint a commander in chief of the army or navy, unless nine States assent to the same: nor shall a question on any other point, except for adjourning from day to day be determined, unless by the votes of the majority of the United States in Congress assembled.

The Congress of the United States shall have power to adjourn to any time within the year, and to any place within the United States, so that no period of adjournment be for a longer duration than the space of six months, and shall publish the journal of their proceedings monthly, except such parts thereof relating to treaties, alliances or military operations, as in their judgement require secrecy; and the yeas and nays of the delegates of each State on any question shall be entered on the journal, when it is desired by any delegates of a State, or any of them, at his or their request shall be furnished with a transcript of the said journal, except such parts as are above excepted, to lay before the legislatures of the several States.

Article X

The Committee of the States, or any nine of them, shall be authorized to execute, in the recess of Congress, such of the powers of Congress as the United States in Congress assembled, by the consent of the nine States, shall from time to time think expedient to vest them with; provided that no power be delegated to the said Committee, for the exercise of which, by the Articles of Confederation, the voice of nine States in the Congress of the United States assembled be requisite.

Article XI

Canada acceding to this confederation, and adjoining in the measures of the United States, shall be admitted into, and entitled to all the advantages of this Union; but no other colony shall be admitted into the same, unless such admission be agreed to by nine States.

Article XII

All bills of credit emitted, monies borrowed, and debts contracted by, or under the authority of Congress, before the assembling of the United States, in pursuance of the present confederation, shall be deemed and considered as a charge against the United States, for payment and satisfaction whereof the said United States, and the public faith are hereby solemnly pledged.

Article XIII

Every State shall abide by the determination of the United States in Congress assembled, on all questions which by this confederation are submitted to them. And the Articles of this Confederation shall be inviolably observed by every State, and the Union shall be perpetual; nor shall any alteration at any time hereafter be made in any of them; unless such alteration be agreed to in a Congress of the United States, and be afterwards confirmed by the legislatures of every State.

And Whereas it hath pleased the Great Governor of the World to incline the hearts of the legislatures we respectively represent in Congress, to approve of, and to authorize us to ratify the said Articles of Confederation and perpetual Union. Know Ye that we the undersigned delegates, by virtue of the power and authority to us given for that purpose, do by these presents, in the name and in behalf of our respective constituents, fully and entirely ratify and confirm each and every of the said Articles of Confederation and perpetual Union, and all and singular the matters and things therein contained: And we do further solemnly plight and engage the faith of our respective constituents, that they shall abide by the determinations of the United States in Congress assembled, on all questions, which by the said Confederation are submitted to them. And that the Articles thereof shall be inviolably observed by the States we respectively represent, and that the Union shall be perpetual.

In Witness whereof we have hereunto set our hands in Congress. Done at Philadelphia in the State of Pennsylvania the ninth day of July in the Year of our Lord One Thousand Seven Hundred and Seventy-Eight, and in the Third Year of the independence of America.

————————————

Agreed to by Congress
15 November 1777
In force after ratification by Maryland, 1 March 1781

FASCINATING FACTS
ABOUT THE SUPREME COURT

★★★★★

When the first session of the Court convened in 1790, the tradition of justices wearing wigs still lingered. Justice William Cushing was the only justice to arrive at the court wearing the white wig he had worn on the Massachusetts bench. The ribbing he took from boys outside the court apparently turned the tide against the headgear, and he took the advice of Thomas Jefferson: "For heaven's sake, discard the monstrous wig which makes the English judges look like rats peeping through bunches of oakum."

★★★★★

During the Supreme Court's first term (1790) it had no docket and made no decisions. When the nation's capital moved to Washington, D. C., in 1800 it did not even have a courtroom. Congress provided a small committee room in the basement of the Capitol, where the Court remained until the Civil War.

★★★★★

In 1789, the chief justice's salary was $4,000, while associate justices made $3,500. By 2013, the chief justice's salary had risen to $223,500, with associate justices receiving $213,900.

★★★★★

The tradition of the "conference handshake" began with Chief Justice Melville W. Fuller in the late 1800s. Before they take their seats at the bench, each justice shakes hands with the others. Chief Justice Fuller cited the practice as a way to remind justices that, although they may have differences of opinion, they share a common purpose.

★★★★★

The longest serving justice was William O. Douglas, who retired in November, 1975, after thirty-six years and six months on the bench. John Rutledge had the briefest Court tenure. He was appointed chief justice and served for four months, at which point the Senate rejected his nomination.

★★★★★

Samuel Chase was the only Supreme Court justice to be impeached. The politically motivated charges failed in the Senate, however, in 1805.

★★★★★

A Supreme Court term begins on the first Monday in October, and runs through late June or early July. The term is divided between "sittings" for the hearing of cases and the delivering of opinions, and intervening "recesses" for the consideration of the business before the Court and the writing of opinions. Sittings and recesses alternate every two weeks or so.

★★★★★

George Washington appointed the most Supreme Court justices (11). Only Franklin D. Roosevelt came close, with 9 appointments.

★★★★★

Two Supreme Court Justices have been featured on U.S. currency: Salmon P. Chase on the $10,000 bill and John Marshall on the $500 bill. Marshall was replaced by William McKinley (the 25th president) before all such bills were discontinued in 1969.

★★★★★

William H. Taft was the only president to also serve as a Supreme Court justice.

★★★★★

Justice Byron ("Whizzer") White is the only justice in the College Football Hall of Fame.

★★★★★

The youngest Supreme Court appointee was Joseph Story (32). The oldest sitting justice was Oliver Wendell Holmes, who served until he was 90.

★★★★★

Jimmy Carter is the only president to serve a full term without nominating a Supreme Court justice.

★★★★★

Of all one-term presidents, Taft appointed the most Supreme Court justices (6).

A SUPREME COURT CASE: HOW IT HAPPENS

GETTING INTO COURT

With few exceptions, the life of a U.S. Supreme Court case begins when a lower court case ends, since the Supreme Court is primarily a court of appeals. The losing party in a lower court case must request entry onto the court's calendar. The justices then decide whether to hear the case, the crucial factor being whether the case can shed new light on an issue of Constitutional law. The Court hears between 75 and 80 of the 10,000 cases that compete for a spot on the court's calendar each year.

PREPARING FOR THE HEARING

Once the court agrees to hear the case, lawyers from each side must submit written arguments. Each justice will typically choose a clerk to review the arguments and prepare a memo, outlining the issues the case presents. The lawyers for each side are told the date of their oral arguments. Shortly before oral arguments, justices review the memos, so they can anticipate each party's argument and the theories behind their reasoning.

INSIDE THE COURTROOM

Each party has one half hour for their oral arguments, including questions from the justices. The justices are seated in order of seniority, with the Chief Justice seated in the center. The next senior justice sits to his right. The next senior justice sits to the Chief Justice's left, and so on, in alternating order. Justices often question the lawyers as their arguments proceed.

THE DECISION

After the oral arguments, there are more arguments, only now they are among the nine justices themselves. They review the case with their clerks (who are recent law school graduates), and chart out an initial impression of their votes. On a day soon thereafter, the justices meet in a conference room, casting their votes. The senior justice on the winning side assigns a justice to the task of writing the majority opinion. That justice will often assign a clerk to prepare a draft of the opinion, usually choosing the clerk who prepared the memo prior to the oral argument. The justice will then use that memo as a basis for writing his or her opinion. The opinion is then passed along to members of the majority, who suggest revisions. Some opinions are revised a dozen or more times before they are announced. When each member of the majority signs off on the opinion, it is ready to be made public. From the bench, the author of the majority opinion will summarize the decision. At that point, the case is forever part of Constitutional law doctrine.

> "We are very quiet there, but it is the quiet of a storm centre."
>
> —JUSTICE OLIVER WENDELL HOLMES,
> SPEAKING OF THE SUPREME COURT

> "[The layman's constitutional view] is that what he likes is constitutional and that which he doesn't like is unconstitutional."
>
> —JUSTICE HUGO L. BLACK

TWENTY LANDMARK CASES IN SUPREME COURT HISTORY

Marbury v. Madison, 1803
"A law repugnant to the Constitution is void."

With these words, Chief Justice John Marshall established the Supreme Court's role in the new government. Hereafter, the Court was recognized as having the power to review all acts of Congress where constitutionality was at issue, and judge whether they abide by the Constitution.

McCulloch v. Maryland, 1819
"Let the end be legitimate … and all means which are … consistent with the letter and spirit of the Constitution, are constitutional."

Chief Justice Marshall invoked this phrase to establish the right of Congress to pass laws that are "necessary and proper" to conduct the business of the U.S. government. Here, the court upheld Congress' power to create a national bank.

Gibbons v. Ogden, 1824
When a federal and state law are in conflict, the federal law is supreme.

Congress and New York had both passed laws regulating the steamboat industry. Gibbons had a federal permit for a steamboat business; Ogden had a state permit for the same waters. Siding with Gibbons, the Court said that, in matters of interstate commerce, the "Supremacy Clause" tilts the balance of power in favor of federal legislation.

Dred Scott v. Sandford, 1857
The Constitution does not consider slaves to be U.S. citizens. Rather, they are constitutionally protected property of their masters.

Chief Justice Roger Taney authored this opinion—one of the most important and scorned in the nation's history. Dred Scott, a slave, had moved with his master to Illinois, a free state. He moved again to a slave state, Missouri, and filed suit to gain freedom, under that state's law of "Once free, always free." Taney held that Scott had never been free at all, and cited Constitutional grounds for placing the slavery decision in the hands of the states. In trying to put an end to the slavery controversy, Taney instead sped the nation toward civil war. The decision was later overturned by the Thirteenth Amendment.

Plessy v. Ferguson, 1896
Jim Crow laws are constitutional under the doctrine of "Separate but Equal."

Police arrested Homer Plessy for refusing to leave a railroad car that prohibited "colored" people. Under Louisiana law, Plessy was "colored" because he was one-eighth black. The Court ruled that the race-based "Jim Crow" laws did not violate the Constitution as long as the states proffered separate but equal treatment.

> *"The Constitution is color blind, and neither knows nor tolerates classes among citizens."*
>
> —JUSTICE JOHN MARSHALL HARLAN, FROM THE LONE DISSENTING OPINION IN PLESSY V. FERGUSON

Lochner v. New York, 1905
The Constitution bars a state from interfering with an employee's right to contract with an employer.

The above reasoning led to the "Lochner Era"— thirty-two years of wrangling between the court and legislatures. Lochner's bakery violated a New York labor law. The court struck down the law, saying that the 14th Amendment's Due Process Clause barred states from regulating commerce in this manner. This clause, the Court said, implied that individuals have a fundamental right to contract with employers, and states cannot interfere with that right.

Near v. Minnesota, 1931
"The liberty of the press ... is safeguarded from invasion by state action."

Although the First Amendment ensures a free press, until this case, it only protected the press from federal laws, not state laws. Minnesota shut down J. M. Near's

Saturday Press for publishing vicious antisemitic and racist remarks. In what is regarded as the landmark free press decision, the Court ruled that a state cannot engage in "prior restraint"; that is, with rare exceptions, it cannot stop a person from publishing or expressing a thought.

West Coast Hotel v. Parrish, 1937
"The switch in time that saved nine."

F. D. R. rallied against the Court's holdings in the Lochner era. The Court struck down New Deal laws, designed to pull the country out of the Depression, on grounds that they interfered with a worker's "right to contract." F. D. R. pledged to expand the Court and pack it with pro "New Deal" members. In this case, the Court rejected the Lochner era decisions and said the government could regulate commerce.

Brown v. Board of Education, 1954
"In the field of public education, the doctrine of 'separate but equal' has no place."

This unanimous decision marked the beginning of the end for the "Separate But Equal" era that started with Plessy, and the start of a new period of American race relations. With Brown, desegregation of public schools began—as did resistance to it. Ten contentious years later, the Civil Rights Act of 1964 made racial equality a matter of federal law.

Mapp v. Ohio, 1961
Evidence that is illegally obtained by the state may not be used against a defendant in court.

Until Mapp, only the federal government was barred from using illegally obtained evidence. So when local police entered Dolly Mapp's home without a search warrant and arrested her for possessing obscene books, her conviction initially stood. The Court overturned her conviction, however, and extended the Constitutional rule to apply to the states and their subdivisions.

> *"I know it when I see it."*
> —JUSTICE POTTER STEWART'S
> DEFINITION OF OBSCENITY
> IN *JACOBELLIS V. OHIO*, 1964

Baker v. Carr, 1962

"One person, one vote."

The above phrase was not authored until a year after Baker, but it has its philosophical roots here. In this case, a group of Tennessee voters sued the state, claiming its voting districts diluted their political power. Until this point, the Court refused to decide this kind of case, leaving such "political questions" to the states. Baker, however, held that the states must meet a Constitutional standard for appointment: districts cannot be drawn in such a way that they violate the Equal Protection clause of the 14th Amendment.

Gideon v. Wainwright, 1963

Defendants in criminal cases have an absolute right to counsel.

Too poor to afford a lawyer, Clarence Earl Gideon was convicted for breaking into a poolroom—a felony crime in Florida. He appealed to the Supreme Court, which ruled that the government must provide free counsel to accused criminals who cannot pay for it themselves. At first, the ruling applied to felonies only. It was later extended to cover any cases where the penalty was six months imprisonment or longer.

New York Times Co. v. Sullivan, 1964

To win a libel case, public figures must prove "actual malice" on the part of the writer.

In 1964, the *Times* published an ad critical of an elected commissioner of an Alabama city. The commissioner sued for libel and won. The Supreme Court overturned that ruling, and said that, to ensure "uninhibited, robust and wide-open" debate about public figures, the law must protect writers from libel suits. Thus, unless the words are penned with "knowing falsity" or "reckless disregard for the truth," a writer cannot be successfully sued by a public figure for libel.

Griswold v. Connecticut, 1965

The Constitution implies a right to privacy in matters of contraception between married people.

Estelle Griswold, the director of a Planned Parenthood clinic, broke an 1879 Connecticut law banning contraception. The Court struck down the law, making it a landmark case in which the Court read the Constitution to protect individual privacy. This was to be the foundation of further privacy rulings, including the right to privacy in matters of abortion.

Miranda v. Arizona, 1966
"You have the right to remain silent ..."

After police questioning, Ernesto Miranda confessed to kidnapping and raping a woman. The Court struck down his conviction, on grounds that he was not informed of his 5th Amendment right against self-incrimination. Hereafter, the Miranda warnings have been a standard feature of arrest procedures.

San Antonio Independent School District v. Rodriguez, 1973
The Constitution does not guarantee a fundamental right to education.

In 1968, a group of low-income parents sued San Antonio, claiming the city's wealthy precincts had better schools. The Court upheld the districting plan, saying that the Constitution did not guarantee an education, and upholding this tenet: The Constitution does not compel government to provide services like education or welfare to the people. Rather, it places boundaries on government action.

Roe v. Wade, 1973
The Constitutionally implied right to privacy protects a woman's choice in matters of abortion.

Norma McCorvey sought an abortion in Texas, but was denied under state law. The Court struck down that law, on grounds that it unconstitutionally restricted the woman's right to choose. The opinion set forth guidelines for state abortion regulations; states could restrict a woman's right to choose only in the later stages of the pregnancy. Later modified but not overruled, the decision stands as one of the Court's most controversial.

United States v. Nixon, 1974

"Neither separation of powers, nor the need for confidentiality can sustain unqualified Presidential immunity from the judicial process."

President Nixon sought precisely this type of immunity, rather than relinquishing the famous White House tapes during the Watergate scandal. The Court unanimously rejected his plea as an unconstitutional power play. The House began impeachment proceedings shortly thereafter, and two weeks after the ruling, Nixon resigned.

Texas v. Johnson, 1989

The Constitution protects desecration of the flag as a form of symbolic speech.

Johnson burned a flag in front of a Dallas building in 1984. He was convicted of violating a Texas law that made it a crime to intentionally desecrate a state or national flag. Justice Brennan wrote for a 5-to-4 majority that "Government may not prohibit the expression of an idea because society finds the idea itself offensive or disagreeable."

Cruzan v. Missouri Dept. of Health, 1990

While the Constitution protects a person's right to reject life-preserving medical treatment (their "right to die"), states can regulate that interest if the regulation is reasonable.

Nancy Cruzan lay in a permanent vegetative state as a result of injuries suffered in an auto accident. Her parents sought to withdraw life-sustaining treatment and allow her to die, claiming she'd said this would be her wish under such circumstances. The state refused, and the Supreme Court upheld the state's guidelines for the continuation of medical treatment, which allowed withdrawal of treatment only with clear and convincing evidence that this is what the patient would have wanted. The Court said that, given the need to protect against abuses of such situations, the state can continue life support as long as its standards for doing so are reasonable.

SUPREME COURT JUSTICES
asterisk denotes chief justice

John Jay* (1789-95)
John Rutledge* (1790-91; 1795)
William Cushing (1790-1810)
James Wilson (1789-98)
John Blair, Jr. (1790-96)
James Iredell (1790-99)
Thomas Johnson (1792-93)
William Paterson (1793-1806)
Samuel Chase (1796-1811)
Olliver Ellsworth* (1796-1800)
Bushrod Washington
  (1799-1829)
Alfred Moore (1800-1804)
John Marshall* (1801-35)
William Johnson (1804-34)
Henry B. Livingston (1807-23)
Thomas Todd (1807-26)
Gabriel Duvall (1811-35)
Joseph Story (1812-45)
Smith Thompson (1823-43)
Robert Trimble (1826-28)
John McLean (1830-61)
Henry Baldwin (1830-44)
James Moore Wayne (1835-67)
Roger B. Taney* (1836-64)
Philip P. Barbour (1836-41)
John Catron (1837-65)
John McKinley (1838-52)
Peter Vivian Daniel (1842-60)
Samuel Nelson (1845-72)
Levi Woodbury (1845-51)
Robert C. Grier (1846-70)
Benjamin R. Curtis (1851-57)
John A. Campbell (1853-61)
Nathan Clifford (1858-81)
Noah Haynes Swayne (1862-81)

Samuel F. Miller (1862-90)
David Davis (1862-77)
Stephen J. Field (1863-97)
Salmon P. Chase* (1864-73)
William Strong (1870-80)
Joseph P. Bradley (1870-92)
Ward Hunt (1873-82)
Morrison R. Waite* (1874-88)
John M. Harlan (1877-1911)
William B. Woods (1881-87)
Stanley Matthews (1881-89)
Horace Gray (1882-1902)
Samuel Blatchford (1882-93)
Lucius Q.C. Lamar (1883-93)
Melville W. Fuller* (1888-1910)
David J. Brewer (1890-1910)
Henry B. Brown (1891-1906)
George Shiras, Jr. (1892-1903)
Howell E. Jackson (1893-95)
Edward D. White* (1894-1921)
Rufus W. Peckham (1896-1909)
Joseph McKenna (1898-1925)
Oliver W. Holmes (1902-32)
William Rufus Day (1903-22)
William H. Moody (1906-10)
Horace H. Lurton (1910-14)
Charles E. Hughes* (1910-16)
Charles E. Hughes* (1930-41)
Willis Van Devanter (1911-37)
Joseph R. Lamar (1911-16)
Mahlon Pitney (1912-22)
James C. McReynolds (1914-41)
Louis D. Brandeis (1916-39)
John H. Clarke (1916-22)
William H. Taft* (1921-30)
George Sutherland (1922-38)

Pierce Butler (1923-39)
Edward T. Sanford (1923-30)
Harlan Fiske Stone* (1925-46)
Owen J. Roberts (1930-45)
Benjamin N. Cardozo (1932-38)
Hugo L. Black (1937-71)
Stanley F. Reed (1938-57)
Felix Frankfurter (1939-62)
William O. Douglas (1939-75)
Frank Murphy (1940-49)
James F. Byrnes (1941-42)
Robert H. Jackson (1941-54)
Wiley B. Rutledge (1943-49)
Harold H. Burton (1945-58)
Fred M. Vinson* (1946-53)
Tom C. Clark (1949-67)
Sherman Minton (1949-56)
Earl Warren* (1953-69)
John M. Harlan (1955-71)
William J. Brennan, Jr. (1956-90)
Charles E. Whittaker (1957-62)
Potter Stewart (1958-81)

Byron R. White (1962-93)
Arthur J. Goldberg (1962-65)
Abe Fortas (1965-69)
Thurgood Marshall (1967-91)
Warren E. Burger* (1969-86)
Harry A. Blackmun (1970-94)
Lewis F. Powell, Jr. (1972-87)
William H. Rehnquist*
   (1972-2005)
John Paul Stevens (1975-2010)
Sandra Day O'Connor
   (1981-2006)
Antonin Scalia (1986-)
Anthony M. Kennedy (1988-)
David Souter (1990-2009)
Clarence Thomas (1991-)
Ruth Bader Ginsburg (1993-)
Stephen G. Breyer (1994-)
John G. Roberts, Jr.* (2005-)
Samuel A. Alito, Jr. (2006-)
Sonia Sotomayor (2009-)
Elena Kagan (2010-)

For more information, including updates to the list of Supreme Court Justices, visit **constitutionfacts.com.**

"It is emphatically the province and duty of the judiciary ... to say what the law is. We must never forget that it is a constitution we are expounding ... intended to endure for ages to come, and consequently, to be adapted to the various crises of human affairs."

—CHIEF JUSTICE JOHN MARSHALL

GLOSSARY

admiralty and maritime law: comes from the general maritime law of nations and has been modified to also apply to the Great Lakes and all navigable rivers in the United States.

amendment: a formal change to the United States Constitution. Currently there are twenty-seven amendments or "changes" to the Constitution.

bad tendency doctrine: allows legislatures to make illegal speech that could encourage people to engage in illegal action.

balanced budget: a philosophy with the objective of not spending more money than is taken in by the government.

bicameral legislature: refers to a two-house legislature.

bill of attainder: a legislative act that authorizes punishment for a person even though he or she was not found guilty by a court of law.

Bill of Rights: the first ten amendments to the Constitution that were adopted in 1791. These are the basic rights that all Americans have and its purpose is to protect the people from the government.

bipartisanship: emphasizes cooperation between the major political parties.

cabinet: a group of governmental officials who head various departments in the Executive Branch and advise the president.

checks and balances: a system set by the Constitution in which the executive, legislative, and judicial branches of government have the power to check each other to maintain a "balance" of power.

clear and present danger: an interpretation of the First Amendment to the Constitution that gives the government the right to curtail activities that may in some way threaten the security of the United States.

cloture: the procedure for ending debate in the United States Senate.

coattail effect: the influence on the outcome of an election that a popular or unpopular candidate has on the other candidates on the same party ticket.

concurrent powers: powers that are shared by the federal government and the state governments.

Constitutional home rule: constitutional authorization for parts of the local government to conduct their own affairs.

cooperative federalism: when the state governments, local governments, and the federal government share responsibility. This has been referred to as the "New Federalism."

crossover voting: this is part of the open primary system in which the voters are not required to vote based upon their party affiliation.

deficit spending: a practice by the government of spending more money than it takes in during a specific time period.

delegated power: powers that are exclusively for the federal government and are "enumerated" in Article I, Section 8 of the Constitution.

democracy: the governmental philosophy in which the people ideally have a high degree of control over political leaders.

detente: a relaxation of tension between countries.

direct democracy: a political process in which the people are able to have direct control over the government in making decisions. In colonial America this was the New England town meeting and today could be exemplified by the referendum.

discharge petition: a petition signed by a majority of the members of the House of Representatives to force a bill from committee and bring it to the floor for consideration.

domestic tranquility: peace at home.

Electoral College: the name for the "indirect" process by which the people elect the president. The "electors" are determined by the number of representatives each state (including Washington, D.C.) has in the House of Representatives and Senate. In a presidential election year the "electors" meet in their respective state capitals on the first Monday after the second Wednesday to "vote" for the President.

ex post facto law: a law that makes an act a crime after it was committed.

exclusionary rule: this is a judicial doctrine based on the Fourth Amendment to the Constitution which protects the American people from illegal searches and seizures. Any evidence obtained in this manner would be inadmissible in a court proceeding.

executive agreement: an agreement between the President of the United States and another country that does not require the advice and consent of the Senate.

executive branch: one of the three branches of our government with the purpose of enforcing laws.

express powers: powers specifically granted to the federal government as enumerated in Article I, Section 8 of the Constitution.

faction: an organized group of politically active persons who are trying to attain special goals. This group is usually less than a majority.

federal supremacy clause: this refers to Article VI, Section 2 of the United States Constitution that states that the Constitution and all federal laws and treaties shall be the "supreme law of the land."

federalism: the division of power between the national government (delegated power) and the state governments (reserved power).

filibuster: the technique used in the United States Senate to delay proceedings and prevent a vote on a controversial issue.

free enterprise: an economic system in which one makes decisions on what products to make, how much of that product to produce, and how to establish the price.

full faith and credit clause: a constitutional provision in Article IV of the Constitution that requires all states to honor the laws, judgments, and public documents of every other state.

gerrymandering: the construction of an election district so as to give a distinct advantage to one party or group over another. This process was named after Elbridge Gerry.

home style: the technique used by a member of Congress to properly present himself/herself to constituents.

House of Representatives: the "lower" house of Congress in which states are represented based on population. Presently there are 435 members in this body.

ideology: an interrelated set of attitudes and beliefs about political philosophy and the role of power in government.

impeachment: a Constitutional "check" the Congress has on the President or other high federal officials. It involves an accusation against that official.

implied power: a power that is not really stated directly but is "implied" in Article I, Section 8, Clause 18 of the Constitution. This is called the "necessary and proper" clause of the "elastic" clause.

impoundment: when the president refuses to allow an agency of the government to spend funds authorized and allocated by Congress.

inalienable rights: the natural rights of all men defined by John Locke as life, liberty, and property that can only be taken away by God. Government is created to protect these rights.

incumbency: one who holds public office that normally carries some type of electoral advantage.

indirect democracy: a political process in which the people control the government through elected political officials. This is also called a republic.

inherent powers: those powers the federal government exercises in foreign affairs which are not specifically stated in the Constitution. They are available because of the status the United States has as a national government.

initiative: the procedure that allows voters to "initiate" legislation by obtaining signatures on a petition.

interstate compact: an agreement among or between states that is approved by Congress.

joint committee: a committee made up of members of both houses of government in order to speed action on the legislation.

judicial branch: one of the three branches of our government with the purpose of interpreting laws.

judicial review: a power the Supreme Court conferred upon itself in the 1803 case of *Marbury v. Madison* (1803) to review the constitutionality of acts passed by Congress or actions by the president.

jus sanguinis: citizenship acquired by citizenship of the parents.

jus soli: citizenship acquired by place of birth.

laissez-faire: a French term meaning to let alone. This infers that the government should not get involved with the peoples' lives.

lame duck: an official who has been defeated in the election but his/her term of office has not expired.

line item veto: the authority of the executive (often the governor) to veto parts of a bill without vetoing the entire piece of legislation.

lobbyist: a person who works for an organized special interest group, association, or corporation. An attempt is made to influence policy decisions primarily in the legislative branch of government.

localism: when states or certain areas tend to act independently and not as a part of the country.

long ballot: originated in the 1820s because of the belief that the voting population should be able to elect all of the officials that govern them.

loose interpretation: a Hamiltonian view of the Constitution that advocates the idea that the federal government has a wide range of powers as implied in Article I, Section 8, Clause 18.

maintaining election: an election that indicates the existence of a pattern of partisan support.

majority floor leader: the legislative position held by an important party member who is chosen by the majority party in caucus or conference. The job is designed to keep members of that party in line and to determine the agenda of that branch of government.

minority floor leader: the party leader in each house of government elected by the minority party.

national debt: the total amount of money the government owes.

National Security Council: a part of the executive branch of government that is a planning and advisory group whose function is to assist the president on matters of national security.

necessary and proper clause: the "implied powers" clause located in Article I, Section 8, Clause 18 of the Constitution. It states that aside from the enumerated powers given to the federal government, it also has the power to pass any law that can be traced back to those powers "delegated" in the Constitution.

nominating convention: a "meeting" in which a political party will choose its candidate for president.

oligarchy: government control is in the hands of a limited number of people who are chosen on the basis of wealth and power.

override: means to "overrule" and refers to the aspect of the "checks and balances" system in which Congress can override a presidential veto by a two-thirds vote.

pocket veto: the constitutional procedure the President may use to prevent a bill from becoming a law without giving specific reasons.

political action committee: a legal organization whose function it is to collect money and make campaign contributions to selected candidates.

political efficacy: the belief that one can have a forceful and meaningful impact on public affairs.

political machine: an organization for running a city or state government by dispensing patronage or favors from the smallest units of government (neighborhood or ward) to the largest. The head of this organization is called a "boss."

poll tax: the requirement that a person must pay a certain amount of money in order to vote. This was found to be unconstitutional in 1964 by the Twenty-Fourth Amendment to the Constitution.

president pro tempore: the senior member of the majority party in the Senate who serves as the president of the Senate when the Vice President is absent.

primary election: an election held to determine the various candidates chosen from each party to run for political office.

prior restraint: limiting First Amendment rights prior to the actual activity that would carry out that freedom (a speech being made, a movie being shown, a newspaper or book being published, etc.)

public domain: the lands held by the state or federal government.

recall election: a special election called by voters to remove an elected official before his/her term expires.

red tape: a way of describing dissatisfaction with the workings of a bureaucracy in terms of inefficiency, mismanagement, and frustration.

referendum: the procedure that allows voters to vote directly on issues instead of going through the "indirect" process of having legislators vote for those issues.

representative government: also known as an "indirect democracy" or a republic. This is when the people elect "representatives" to make laws for their benefit.

republic: the type of government in which voters elect representatives to make the laws for the country.

reserved power: powers that are "reserved" for the states as identified in the Tenth Amendment to the Constitution.

retrospective voting: voting that takes into consideration such things as the performance of the political party, the officeholder, and/or the administration.

safe seat: an elected office where the party in power or the incumbent is so strong that being reelected is a foregone conclusion.

sedition: the attempt to overthrow a government by force or at least interrupt its activities.

Senate: one of the two houses of Congress historically known as the "upper" house that contains two representatives from each state regardless of population. Presently there are 100 members in this body.

Senatorial courtesy: the custom in the United States Senate to refer the names of possible appointees (specifically federal judges) to senators from the states from which the appointee reside and withdrawing the names of those appointees that these senators regard as objectionable.

separation of powers: the philosophy of a balanced government in which each of the three branches (executive, legislative, judicial) have their own powers.

socialism: a type of government that believes its major role should be on the concentration of national planning and public ownership of business.

sovereignty: the source of a government's power or authority.

Speaker of the House: the presiding officer of the United States House of Representatives who is selected by a caucus of his/her party and is formally elected by the entire House.

spoils system: the practice of rewarding those who worked in a successful political campaign by giving them governmental jobs.

standing committee: the name given to a permanent congressional committee.

states' rights: the belief that the individual states had/have more power than the federal government.

strict interpretation: a Jeffersonian view of the Constitution that advocates the idea that the federal government has only those powers as identified in Article I, Section 8.

suffrage: The right or privilege of voting.

ticket splitting: the practice of voting for candidates without taking into consideration their political affiliation.

totalitarian government: the type of government that is characterized by a single party or individual controlling the entire country and every aspect of society.

tyranny: description of a government that is cruel or unjust.

unconstitutional: a legislative act or presidential action that violates the Constitution based on the interpretation of the Supreme Court.

unicameral legislature: refers to a one-house legislature.

unitary system: a type of government that concentrates power in the central government.

unite rule: a rule that the entire delegation to a party convention must cast its vote based upon the rule of the majority.

veto: to reject or refuse to sign a bill from Congress. This is the "check" that the president has on the powers of the legislative branch of government

Whip: the party leader who is the "intermediary" between the leadership and the rank and file in the legislature.

INDEX TO THE U.S. CONSTITUTION & AMENDMENTS

94